P9-BBQ-576

THE QUOTABLE EINSTEIN

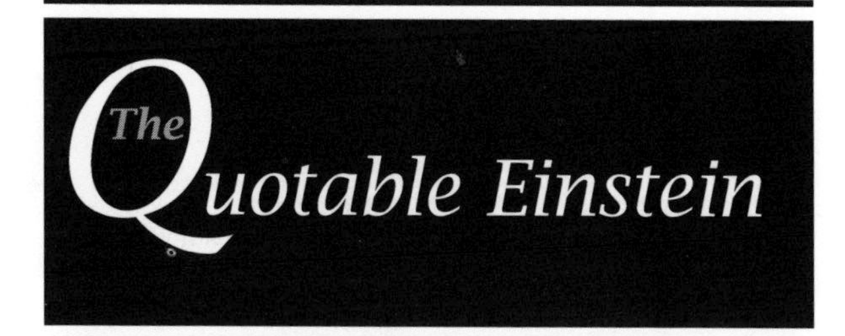

COLLECTED AND EDITED BY

Alice Calaprice

WITH A FOREWORD BY

Freeman Dyson

PRINCETON UNIVERSITY PRESS

PRINCETON, NEW JERSEY

Published by Princeton University Press, 41 William Street,
Princeton, New Jersey 08540
In the United Kingdom: Princeton University Press,
Chichester, West Sussex

Library of Congress Cataloging-in-Publication Data

Einstein, Albert, 1879–1955.
The quotable Einstein / collected and edited by
Alice Calaprice ; with a foreword by Freeman Dyson.
p. cm.
Includes bibliographical references and indexes.
ISBN 0-691-02696-3 (cloth : alk. paper)
1. Einstein, Albert, 1879–1955—Quotations.
I. Calaprice, Alice. II. Title.
QC16.E5A25 1996
081—dc20 96-3543

This book has been composed in Palatino

Princeton University Press books are printed on
acid-free paper and meet the guidelines for permanence
and durability of the Committee on Production
Guidelines for Book Longevity of the
Council on Library Resources

http://pup.princeton.edu

Printed in the United States of America

10 9 8 7 6

Frontispiece: Einstein relaxing at Huntington, Long Island,
1937. (Lotte Jacobi Archives, University of New Hampshire)

Contents

Foreword

My excuse for writing this foreword is that I have been for thirty years a friend and adviser to Princeton University Press, helping to smooth the way for the huge and difficult project of publishing the Einstein Papers, a project in which Alice Calaprice is playing a central role. After long delays and bitter controversies, the publication project is now going full steam ahead, producing a steady stream of volumes packed with scientific and historical treasures.

I knew Einstein only at second hand through his secretary and keeper of the archives, Helen Dukas. Helen was a warm and generous friend to grownups and children alike. She was for many years our children's favorite babysitter. She loved to tell stories about Einstein, always emphasizing his sense of humor and his serene detachment from the passions that agitate lesser mortals. Our children remember her as a gentle and good-humored old lady with a German accent. But she was also tough. She fought like a tiger to keep out people who tried to intrude upon Einstein's privacy while he was alive, and she fought like a tiger to preserve the privacy of his more intimate papers after he died. She and Otto Nathan were the executors of Einstein's will, and they stood ready with lawsuits to punish anyone who tried to publish Einstein documents without their approval. Underneath Helen's serene surface we could occasionally sense the hidden tensions. She would sometimes mutter darkly about unnamed people who were making her life miserable.

Einstein's will directed that the archive containing his papers should remain under the administration of Otto Nathan and Helen so long as they lived, and should thereafter belong permanently to the Hebrew University in Jerusalem. For twenty-six years after Einstein's death in 1955, the archive was housed in a long row of filing cabinets at the Institute for Advanced Study in Princeton. Helen worked every day at the archive, carrying on an enormous correspondence and discovering thousands of new documents to add to the collection.

In December 1981, Otto Nathan and Helen were both in apparently good health. Then, one night around Christmas, when most of the Institute members were on holiday, there was a sudden move. It was a dark and rainy night. A large truck stood in front of the Institute with a squad of well-armed Israeli soldiers standing guard. I happened to be passing by and waited to see what would happen. I was the only visible spectator, but I have little doubt that Helen was also present, probably supervising the operation from her window on the top floor of the Institute. In quick succession, a number of big wooden crates were brought down in the elevator from the top floor, carried out of the building through the open front door, and loaded onto the truck. The soldiers jumped on board and the truck drove away into the night. The next day, the archive was in its final resting place in Jerusalem. Helen continued to come to work at the Institute, taking care of her correspondence and tidying up the empty space where the archive had been. Six weeks later, suddenly and unexpectedly, she died. We never knew whether she had had a premonition of her death; in any case, she made sure that her beloved archive would be in safe hands before her departure.

After the Hebrew University took responsibility for the archive and after Otto Nathan's death in January 1987, the ghosts that had been haunting Helen quickly emerged into daylight. Robert Schulmann, a historian of science who had joined the Einstein Papers Project a few years earlier, received a tip from Switzerland that a secret cache of love letters, written around the turn of the century by Einstein and his first wife, Mileva Marić, might still exist. He began to suspect that the cache might be part of Mileva's literary estate, brought to California by her daughter-in-law Frieda, the first wife of Einstein's older son, Hans, after Mileva's death in Switzerland in 1948. Though Schulmann had received repeated assurances that the only extant letters were those dating from after Mileva's separation from Einstein in 1914, he was not convinced. He met in 1986 with Einstein's granddaughter, Evelyn, in Berkeley. Together they discovered a critical clue. Tucked away in an unpublished manuscript that Frieda had prepared about Mileva, but not part of the text, were notes referring with great immediacy to fifty-four love letters. The conclusion was obvious. These letters must be part of the group of more than four hundred in the hands of the Einstein Family Correspondence Trust, the legal entity representing Mileva's California heirs. Because Otto Nathan and Helen Dukas had earlier blocked publication of Frieda's biography, the Family Trust had denied them access to this correspondence and they had no direct knowledge of its contents. The discovery of Frieda's notes and the transfer of the literary estate to Hebrew University afforded a new opportunity to pursue publication of the correspondence.

In spring 1986, John Stachel, at the time the editor responsible for the publication of the archive, and Reuven Yaron, of the Hebrew University, broke the logjam by negotiating a settlement with the Family Trust. Their aim was to have photocopies of the correspondence deposited with the publication project and with the Hebrew University. The crucial meeting took place in California, where Thomas Einstein, the physicist's oldest great-grandson and a trustee of the Family Trust, lives. The negotiators were disarmed when the young man arrived in tennis shorts, and a friendly settlement was quickly reached. As a result, the intimate letters became public. The letters to Mileva revealed Einstein as he really was, a man not immune from normal human passions and weaknesses. The letters are masterpieces of pungent prose, telling the old sad story of a failed marriage, beginning with tender and playful love, ending with harsh and cold withdrawal.

During the years when Helen ruled over the archive, she kept by her side a wooden box which she called her "Zettelkästchen"—her little box of snippets. Whenever in her daily work she came across an Einstein quote that she found striking or charming, she typed her own copy of it and put it in the box. When I visited her in her office, she would always show me the latest additions to the box. The contents of the box became the core of the book *Albert Einstein, the Human Side,* an anthology of Einstein quotes which she co-edited with Banesh Hoffmann and published in 1979. *The Human Side* depicts the Einstein that Helen wanted the world to see, the Einstein of legend, the friend of schoolchildren and impoverished students, the gently ironic philosopher, the Einstein without violent feelings and tragic mistakes. It is interesting to contrast the Einstein portrayed by Helen in *The Human Side* with the Einstein portrayed by Alice Calaprice in this book. Alice has chosen her quotes impartially from the old and the new documents. She does not emphasize the darker side of Einstein's personality, and she does not conceal it. In the brief section "On Family," for example, the darker side is clearly revealed.

In writing a foreword to this collection, I am forced to confront the question whether I am committing an act of betrayal. It is clear that Helen would have vehemently opposed the publication of the intimate letters to Mileva and to Einstein's second wife, Elsa. She would probably have felt betrayed if she had seen my name attached to a book that contained many quotes from the letters that she abhorred. I was one of her close and trusted friends, and it is not easy for me to go against her express wishes. If I am betraying her, I do not do so lightheartedly. In the end, I salve my conscience with the thought that she was, in spite of her many virtues, profoundly wrong in trying to hide the true Einstein from the world. While she was alive, I never pretended to agree with her on this point. I did not try to change her mind, because her conception of her duty to Einstein was unchangeable, but I made it clear to her that I disliked the use of lawsuits to stop publication of Einstein documents. I had enormous love and respect for Helen as a person, but I never promised that I would support her policy of censorship. I hope and almost believe that, if Helen were now alive and could see with her own eyes that the universal admiration and respect for Einstein have not been diminished by the publication of his intimate letters, she would forgive me.

It is clear to me now that the publication of the intimate letters, even if it is a betrayal of Helen Dukas, is not a betrayal of Einstein. Einstein emerges from this collection of quotes, drawn from many different sources, as a complete and fully rounded human being, a greater and more astonishing figure than the tame philosopher portrayed in Helen's book. Knowledge of the darker side of Einstein's life makes his achievements in science and in public affairs even more miraculous. This book shows him as he was—not a superhuman genius but a human genius, and all the greater for being human.

A few years ago I had the good luck to be lecturing in Tokyo at the same time as the cosmologist Stephen Hawking. Walking the streets of Tokyo with Hawking in his wheelchair was an amazing experience. I felt as if I were taking a walk through Galilee with Jesus Christ. Everywhere we went, crowds of Japanese silently streamed after us, stretching out their hands to touch Hawking's wheelchair. Hawking enjoyed the spectacle with detached good humor. I was thinking of an account that I had read of Einstein's visit to Japan in 1922. The crowds had streamed after Einstein then as they streamed after Hawking seventy years later. The Japanese people worshiped Einstein as they now worshiped Hawking. They showed exquisite taste in their choice of heroes. Across the barriers of culture and language, they sensed a godlike quality in these two visitors from afar. Somehow they understood that Einstein and Hawking were not just great scientists but great human beings. This book helps to explain why.

Freeman Dyson
THE INSTITUTE FOR ADVANCED STUDY
PRINCETON, NEW JERSEY

Preface and Acknowledgments

> In the past it never occurred to me that every casual remark of mine would be snatched up and recorded. Otherwise I would have crept further into my shell.
>
> —*Einstein to his biographer Carl Seelig, October 25, 1953*

Albert Einstein was a prolific—and often thoughtful and gifted—writer, and he is immensely quotable. This I discovered when I began my work with the Einstein papers in 1978 preparing a computerized index of the duplicate Einstein archive, located at the time (along with the original archive) at the Institute for Advanced Study in Princeton. The job, under the direction of John Stachel, then the editor of *The Collected Papers of Albert Einstein*, required a perusal of all the documents—correspondence, writings, and third-party commentary. From these an assistant and I would glean certain bits of information and enter them into the not-so-user-friendly computer of the 1970s that was made available to us at the Princeton University cyclotron lab. I would often read these items—most of them in German—more thoroughly than necessary, simply because they were so engrossing. I impulsively began to keep an index-card file of my favorite excerpts and quotations, and these cards are now, at long last, serving as the basis for this book.

Since I came to work at Princeton University Press and was appointed both in-house editor of the Press's huge publishing venture, *The Collected Papers of Albert Einstein*, and administrator of its accompanying translation project, I have often received calls and letters from people asking for the source of this quotation or that, usually found on some calendar or heard on the radio and attributed to Einstein. At the same time, I have learned that the Einstein Project editorial offices in Boston, the Firestone Library at Princeton University, and the library at the Institute for Advanced Study have also been besieged with such inquiries; and most of the time we have not been able—at least not easily or quickly—to establish the source or correct quotation. This situation, the blue plastic box of quotations on my shelf, and the interest of Trevor Lipscombe, the Press's physical sciences editor, gave me the idea for this book.

To come up with this selection, I have not only depended on my blue box but also searched through many other original sources plus Einstein biographies and additional secondary sources, as well as rechecked parts of the duplicate archive. I have not limited myself to quotations suitable for after-dinner speeches and epigraphs but have also included some less profound utterings that reflect various facets of Einstein's personality. Some of these may distress readers who have worshiped Einstein as a compassionate, tolerant, and flawless hero (see, for instance, his brusque reply to a Chilean official who requested some words of wisdom, his diary entry regarding the devout at the Wailing Wall in Jerusalem, and his ideas on women in science). Other readers may take pleasure in the fact that their worst prejudices against him, whether they be religious, philosophical, or political, are confirmed by his thoughts on abortion, marriage, communism, and world government. Still others will delight in his humor (see, for instance, the subsection on animals and pets under "Miscellaneous Subjects"), and will identify with him as he shares his thoughts on everything from youth to aging, from pipe smoking to going sockless.

But before rushing to judgment, one must take into consideration Einstein's age at the time of quotation and his milieu—the historical and cultural times in which he lived. Indeed, over his lifetime, he changed his mind or qualified his opinion on several topics—pacifism, the death penalty, and Zionism, for instance. In addition, although he used the now politically incorrect *mankind* and generic *he* when referring to people in general, professionally he did dwell in a man's world. Moreover, much of the use of *man* may be due to mistranslations of the German *Mensch*, which refers collectively to men and women.

The organization of the book fell naturally into the categories listed alphabetically (after the section "On Einstein Himself") in the table of contents, and then into a larger "Miscellaneous" section, also organized alphabetically by subject. Within each category, the quotations are listed chronologically when I was able to find the dates of the quotations, and then the remaining ones in that category are somewhat lumped together by sources that did not give a date.

I quote from the original documents whenever possible. Among these are the Einstein archive (I give the document numbers of the duplicate archives found in Princeton and Boston); the volumes in *The Collected Papers of Albert Einstein* (*CPAE*); *Albert Einstein, the Human Side* by Helen Dukas and Banesh Hoffmann, which contains archival material selected by Einstein's secretary who was also his longtime archivist; and the various books and journals in which certain articles first appeared. In addition, I often list as well more easily available yet reliable compilations such as *Ideas and Opinions*, so that readers can consult this more popular literature for the complete text and context. (My page numbers refer to the editions cited in the Bibliography.) In the few instances where I could not find an original source, I relied on the secondary literature such as biographies.

I have made every effort to verify references, but *The Quotable Einstein* cannot aspire to be a work of scholarship in the strictest sense—I cannot claim to have used the best or most authoritative version of a translation, for example, as these often differ from book to book. If I found no translation, I relied on my own German, or that of friends.

Needless to say, there must be many worthy words that I did not come across (and that are hiding somewhere among the over 40,000 documents in the archive), so this first effort can by no means be considered a complete book of quotations. But I hope that, for now, I have been able to present and document the most important or interesting ones. As this will be an ongoing project, with enlarged editions (including, when possible, the original German versions of the writings) published every few years, I invite the reader to send me any quotations, along with their sources, that I have missed. We will include these in the future editions. If I have inadvertently misquoted Einstein or given a false source, let me know that as well.

I came across a few quotations whose sources I could not find, yet I—or people who have called me with inquiries—have seen or heard them attributed to Einstein. I have put these at the back of the book in a small section entitled "Attributed to Einstein";

my hope is that readers can lead me to the proper documentation.

To help the reader or researcher locate items, I have compiled two indexes: an Index of Key Words will help readers find familiar quotations, and the Subject Index will lead them to subjects of particular interest.

Finally, I wish to record my acknowledgments to those who have helped in the preparation of this book. First, I thank the Hebrew University of Jerusalem for permission to include material from the Einstein archive, Philosophical Library for permission to include material reprinted in *Ideas and Opinions*, and Crown Publishers for permission to use the quotations drawn from Jamie Sayen's *Einstein in America*. I thank Larry McCallister of Viacom/Paramount Pictures for kindly waiving the permissions fee for use of the photograph of Walter Matthau portraying Einstein in the motion picture *I.Q.*

I am also grateful for the help, interest, and support of my family, friends, and colleagues. In particular, I would like to thank my colleagues at Princeton University Press who have shown enthusiasm for this project from the start, especially Trevor Lipscombe, Eric Rohmann, and Emily Wilkinson. In addition, special thanks go to my longtime friend and our managing editor, Janet Stern, for showing me that even a professional editor's writing needs to be edited. Computer whiz Linda Moran patiently initiated me into the world of WordPerfect, then showed great proficiency in composing this book. Our senior designer, Jan Lilly, designed the book with sensitivity and skill. Bing Lin Zhao of Boston University remained good-natured and uncommonly helpful when I repeatedly interrupted his work to enlist his help in computer searches, saving me hours of time. Evelyn Einstein graciously helped me update the Einstein family tree, and Mark Hazarabedian designed it with great care. My mother, Rusan Abeghian, clipped Einstein material from newspapers in several languages.

I am also grateful to Freeman Dyson for taking time out from his busy schedule to write the foreword, even though he would have preferred seeing the original German in this volume as well. When I was looking through my old index cards, I came across one on which I had scribbled some remarks that Helen Dukas had made about him in 1978. Helen, who knew I was of half-Armenian descent, had told me about an article that Freeman, whom I had not yet met, had written for the *New Yorker* several years earlier about his visit to Armenia. After our discussion she said something more about Freeman Dyson that is worthy of quotation in a book such as this: "He is a great man. My one regret is that he did not meet Professor Einstein. In the '50s the professor mentioned that he had heard of this interesting young man. I told him I could arrange a meeting, but the professor said, 'Oh, no, I don't want to bother such an important man!'" Unlike the polite Professor Einstein, I dared to bother this man—to ask him to write a foreword for this book; and I am deeply grateful that he readily agreed.

Last but not least, Robert Schulmann, director of the Einstein Papers Project at Boston University, has, as always, been an invaluable friend and source of information and good cheer, even when I felt that I was testing his patience. I hope that this little book has met everyone's expectations.

PRINCETON
JANUARY 1996

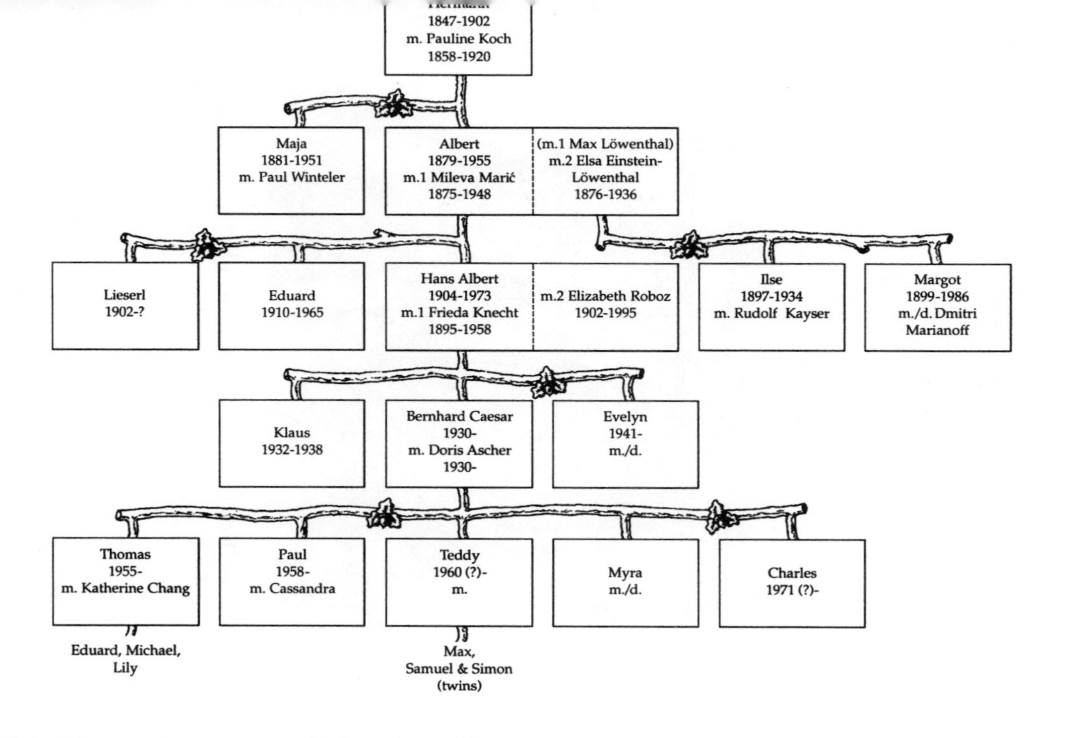

1847-1902
m. Pauline Koch
1858-1920
Maja
1881-1951
m. Paul Winteler
Albert
1879-1955
m.1 Mileva Marić
1875-1948
(m.1 Max Löwenthal)
m.2 Elsa Einstein-
Löwenthal
1876-1936
Lieserl
1902-?
Eduard
1910-1965
Hans Albert
1904-1973
m.1 Frieda Knecht
1895-1958
m.2 Elizabeth Roboz
1902-1995
Ilse
1897-1934
m. Rudolf Kayser
Margot
1899-1986
m./d. Dmitri
Marianoff
Klaus
1932-1938
Bernhard Caesar
1930-
m. Doris Ascher
1930-
Evelyn
1941-
m./d.
Thomas
1955-
m. Katherine Chang
Paul
1958-
m. Cassandra
Teddy
1960 (?)-
m.
Myra
m./d.
Charles
1971 (?)-
Eduard, Michael,
Lily
Max,
Samuel & Simon
(twins)

In Bern, ca. 1905. (Courtesy of Lotte Jacobi Archives, University of New Hampshire)

Chronology

This chronology was assembled primarily from information contained in the chronologies of volumes 1 and 5 of the *Collected Papers of Albert Einstein*; from the chronology in *Subtle Is the Lord* by Abraham Pais; and from my notes of conversations with Helen Dukas in 1978–80. It was supplemented by data gathered from additional readings.

1879 March 14, Albert Einstein is born in Ulm, Germany, in the home of his parents, Hermann (1847–1902) and Pauline Koch (1858–1920) Einstein.

1880 Family moves to Munich.

1881 November 18, Einstein's sister Maja is born.

1884 Receives from his father a compass, which makes a great impression on the young child.

1885 In the fall, enters the Petersschule, a Catholic primary school, where he is the only Jew in class. Receives Jewish religious instruction at home and becomes curious about religion; his religiosity ends by age twelve. Begins violin lessons.

1888 Enters Luitpold-*Gymnasium* in Munich.

1889–1895 Interest in physics, mathematics, and philosophy develops.

1894 Family moves to Italy, but Albert stays in Munich to finish school. He quits the *Gymnasium* at the end of the year and joins his family in Italy.

1895 Attempts to enter the Federal Polytechnical Institute (now the ETH—Eidgenössische Technische Hochschule) in Zurich in the fall, two years before the regular age of admission, but fails the entrance exam. Instead, attends the Aargau Cantonal School in Aarau while living in the home of one of his teachers, Jost Winteler, and his family.

1896 Relinquishes his German citizenship due to his dislike of the German military mentality and remains stateless for the next five years. In the fall, is graduated from the Aargau school, entitling him to enter the Federal Polytechnical Institute, and he moves to Zurich at the end of October.

1899 Applies for Swiss citizenship at the age of twenty.

1900 Is graduated from the Polytechnical Institute, but his application to become an assistant at the Poly for the fall semester is turned down. In the summer, tells his disapproving mother that he plans to marry fellow student Mileva Marić. At end of year, sends his first scientific paper to *Annalen der Physik*.

1901 Becomes a Swiss citizen. Seeks employment. His first scientific paper, "Conclusions Drawn from the Phenomena of Capillarity," is published in March. In the summer, works as a substitute teacher at the technical school in Winterthur, and in the fall as a tutor at a private boarding school in Schaffhausen. Stays in touch with and visits Mileva regularly. Begins work on a doctoral dissertation on molecular forces in gases, which he submits to the University of Zurich in November. December, applies for a position at the Swiss Patent Office in Bern.

1902 Probably in January, daughter Lieserl is born out of wedlock to Mileva. Withdraws his doctoral dissertation from the University of Zurich. June, begins a provisional appointment as Technical Expert, Third Class, at the Patent Office in Bern. Father dies in October in Milan.

1903 January 6, marries Mileva in Bern, where they take up residence. September, daughter Lieserl is registered, which may have indicated intention to put her up for adoption in case knowledge of the illegitimacy would be a threat to Einstein's federal appointment. No mention is made of Lieserl after she comes down with scarlet fever in September while Mileva is on a visit to Budapest. (It appears that Lieserl never lived with her parents, and all trace of her has been lost.) At this time Mileva is also pregnant again.

1904 May 14, son Hans Albert is born in Bern (died 1973 in Falmouth, Massachusetts). September, Einstein's provisional appointment at the Patent Office becomes permanent.

1905 Einstein's "year of miracles" with respect to his scientific publications. April 30, submits his doctoral dissertation, "A New Determination of Molecular Dimensions," for publication. In addition, publishes three of his most important scientific papers: "On a Heuristic Point of View Concerning the Production and Transformation of Light" (published June 9), which deals with the quantum hypothesis, showing that electromagnetic radiation interacts with matter as if the radiation has a granular structure (the so-called photoelectric effect); "On the Movement of Small Particles

Suspended in Stationary Liquids Required by the Molecular-Kinetic Theory of Heat" (published July 18), his first paper on Brownian motion, leading to experiments validating the kinetic-molecular theory of heat; and "On the Electrodynamics of Moving Bodies" (published September 26), his first paper on the special theory of relativity and a landmark in the development of modern physics. A second, shorter paper on the special theory, published November 21, contains the relation $E = mc^2$ in its original form (see quotation under $E = mc^2$ in the section "On Science and Scientists, Mathematics, and Technology").

1906 January 15, formally receives doctorate from the University of Zurich. March 10, promoted to Technical Expert, Second Class, at the Patent Office.

1907 While still at the Patent Office, seeks other employment, including at the cantonal school in Zurich and at the University of Bern.

1908 February, becomes a *Privatdozent* (lecturer) at the University of Bern. Sister Maja receives her doctorate in romance languages from the University of Bern.

1909 May 7, is appointed Extraordinary Professor of Theoretical Physics at the University of Zurich, effective October 15. Resigns from his positions at the Swiss Patent Office and the University of Bern. Receives his first honorary doctorate, from the University of Geneva.

1910 March, sister Maja marries Paul Winteler, son of Einstein's teacher in Aargau. July 28, second son, Eduard, is born (died 1965 in a psychiatric hospital in Burghölzli). October, completes a paper on critical opalescence and the blue color of the sky, his last major work in classical statistical physics.

1911 Accepts an appointment as director of the Institute of Theoretical Physics at the German University of Prague, effective April 1, and resigns his position at the University of Zurich. Moves his family to Prague. October 29, attends the first Solvay Congress in Brussels.

1912 Becomes acquainted with his divorced cousin Elsa Löwenthal and begins a romantic correspondence with her as his own marriage disintegrates. Accepts appointment as Professor of Theoretical Physics at the ETH in Zurich, beginning in October, and resigns his position in Prague.

1913 September, sons Hans Albert and Eduard are baptized as Orthodox Christians near Novi Sad, Yugoslavia, their mother's hometown. November, is elected to the Prussian Academy of Sciences and is offered a position in Berlin, home of Elsa Löwenthal. The offer includes a research professorship at the University of Berlin, without teaching obligations, and the directorate of the soon-to-be-established Kaiser Wilhelm Institute of Physics. Resigns from the ETH.

1914 April, arrives in Berlin to assume his new position. Mileva and the children join him but soon return to Zurich due to Mileva's unhappiness in Berlin. August, World War I begins.

1915 Co-signs a "Manifesto to Europeans" upholding European culture, probably his first public political statement. November, completes his work on the logical structure of general relativity.

1916 Publishes "The Origins of the General Theory of Relativity" (later to become his first book) in *Annalen der Physik*. May, becomes president of the German Physical Society. Publishes three papers on quantum theory.

1917 February, writes his first paper on cosmology. Becomes ill and is weakened by a liver ailment and an ulcer. Elsa takes care of him. October 1, begins directorship of the Kaiser Wilhelm Institute of Physics. After World War I, holds dual Swiss and German citizenship.

1919 February 14, is divorced from Mileva. Divorce decree stipulates that any future Nobel Prize monies will go to her and the children for living expenses. May 29, during a solar eclipse Sir Arthur Eddington experimentally measures the bending of light and confirms Einstein's predictions; Einstein's fame as a public figure begins. June 2, marries Elsa, who has two unmarried daughters, Ilse (22 years old) and Margot (20 years old), living at home. Late in the year becomes interested in Zionism through his friendship with Kurt Blumenfeld.

1920 March, mother Pauline dies in Berlin. Expressions of anti-Semitism and anti–relativity theory become noticeable among Germans, yet Einstein remains loyal to Germany. Becomes increasingly involved in nonscientific interests.

1921 April and May, makes first trip to the United States. Delivers four lectures on relativity theory at Princeton University and receives honorary doctorate. Accompanies Chaim Weizmann on U.S. fund-raising tour on behalf of Hebrew University of Jerusalem.

1922 Completes his first paper on a unified field theory. October through December, takes trip to Japan, with other stops en route to the Far East. November, announcement that Einstein has won the 1921 Nobel Prize in physics for his "services to theoretical physics and especially for his discovery of the photoelectric effect"; many considered this a consolation prize because it was not given specifically for the increasingly controversial theory of relativity. Princeton University Press in the United States and Methuen and Company in Great Britain publish *The Meaning of Relativity*, based on Princeton University's Stafford Little Lectures of 1921.

1923 Visits Palestine and Spain.

1924 Stepdaughter Ilse marries Rudolf Kayser.

1925 Travels to South America. In solidarity with Gandhi, signs a manifesto against compulsory universal military service. Becomes an ardent pacifist. Receives Copley Medal. Until 1928, serves on Board of Governors of Hebrew University.

1926 Royal Astronomical Society of England awards him its gold medal.

1927 Son Hans Albert marries Frieda Knecht.

1928 Falls ill again, this time with a heart problem. Is confined to bed for several months and remains weak for a year. April, Helen Dukas is hired as his secretary and remains with him the rest of his life.

1929 Begins lifelong friendship with Queen Elizabeth of Belgium. June, receives Planck Medal.

1930 First grandchild, Bernhard, is born to Hans Albert and Frieda. Stepdaughter Margot marries Dmitri

Marianoff (marriage later ends in divorce). Signs manifesto for world disarmament. December, visits New York and Cuba and stays (until March 1931) at the California Institute of Technology (CalTech), Pasadena.

1931 Visits Oxford in May, then spends several months at his summer cottage at Caputh, southwest of Berlin. December, en route to Pasadena again.

1932 January–March, visits CalTech again. Returns to Berlin. Later, agrees to accept an appointment as professor at the Institute for Advanced Study in Princeton, to begin when its campus is completed. December, makes another visit to the United States.

1933 January, Nazis come to power. Resigns membership in the Prussian Academy of Sciences, gives up German citizenship (remains a Swiss citizen), and does not return to Germany. Instead, from the U.S., goes to Belgium with Elsa and sets up temporary residence at Coq-sur-Mer. Ilse, Margot, Helen Dukas, and Walther Mayer, an assistant, join them, and security guards are assigned to protect them. Takes trips to Oxford and Switzerland, where he makes what will be his final visit to son Eduard. Rudolf Kayser, Ilse's husband, manages to have Einstein's papers in Berlin sent to France and eventually brought to the United States. September, leaves Europe, together with Elsa, Helen Dukas, and Walther Mayer, and arrives in New York on October 17 on the *Westmoreland*; Ilse and Margot and their spouses remain in Europe. Publishes, with Sigmund Freud, *Why War?* Begins professorship at the Institute for Advanced Study, temporarily located in the old Fine

Hall (now Jones Hall) on the Princeton University campus.

1934 July 10, Ilse dies in Paris after a long and painful illness. Margot and Dmitri come to Princeton.

1935 Fall, moves to 112 Mercer Street, Princeton, where Einstein, Elsa, Margot, and Helen Dukas live out their lives. Receives the Franklin Medal.

1936 Hans Albert receives a doctorate in technical sciences from the ETH in Zurich (in 1947 he becomes a professor of hydraulic engineering at the University of California at Berkeley). December 20, Elsa dies after a long battle with heart and kidney disease.

1939 Sister Maja Einstein-Winteler comes to live at Mercer Street. August 2, signs famous letter to President Roosevelt on the military implications of atomic energy. World War II begins in Europe.

1940 Receives U.S. citizenship. Maintains dual U.S. and Swiss citizenship until his death. Citizenship had been proposed earlier by an act of Congress, but Einstein preferred waiting to be naturalized the usual way.

1941 United States enters World War II.

1943 Becomes consultant to U.S. Navy Bureau of Ordnance, Section on Explosives and Ammunition.

1944 A newly handwritten copy of the original 1905 paper on the special theory of relativity is auctioned off for $6 million as a contribution to the war effort.

1945 World War II ends. Retires officially from the faculty of the Institute for Advanced Study, receives a pension, but continues to keep an office there until his death.

1946 Maja suffers a stroke and is confined to bed. Einstein becomes chairman of the Emergency Committee of Atomic Scientists. Urges United Nations to form a world government, declaring that it is the only way to maintain permanent peace.

1948 August 4, Mileva dies in Zurich. December, Einstein's doctors tell him that he has a large aneurysm of the abdominal aorta.

1950 March 18, signs his last will, naming Otto Nathan as executor and Otto Nathan and Helen Dukas as trustees of his estate. His literary estate (the archive) is to be transferred to the Hebrew University of Jerusalem after the death of Nathan and Dukas. (Arrangements are later made for an earlier transfer.)

1951 June, Maja dies in Princeton.

1952 Is offered the presidency of Israel, which he declines.

1954 Develops hemolytic anemia.

1955 April 11, writes last signed letter, to Bertrand Russell, agreeing to sign a joint manifesto urging all nations to renounce nuclear weapons. April 13, aneurysm ruptures. April 15, enters Princeton Hospital. April 18, Albert Einstein dies at 1:15 A.M. of a ruptured arteriosclerotic aneurysm of the abdominal aorta.

THE QUOTABLE EINSTEIN

On Einstein Himself

In Princeton, 1938. (Lotte Jacobi Archives, University of New Hampshire)

A happy man is too satisfied with the present to dwell too much on the future.

Written at age 17 (September 18, 1896) for a school French examination entitled "My Future Plans"; *CPAE*, Vol. 1, Doc. 22

I decided the following about our future: I will look *immediately* for a position, no matter how humble. My scientific goals and my personal vanity will not prevent me from accepting the most subordinate role.

Letter to future wife Mileva Marić, July 7, 1901, while having difficulty finding his first job; *CPAE*, Vol. 1, Doc. 114

I have come to know the mutability of all human relations and have learned to isolate myself from heat and cold so that the temperature balance is fairly well assured.

Letter to Heinrich Zangger, March 10, 1917; Einstein Archive 39-680

Here is yet another application of the principle of relativity . . . : today I am described in Germany as a "German savant" and in England as a "Swiss

Jew." Should it ever be my fate to be represented as a bête noire, I should, on the contrary, become a "Swiss Jew" for the Germans and a "German savant" for the English.

Letter to *The Times* (London), 1919, quoted in Hoffmann, *Albert Einstein: Creator and Rebel*, p. 139; also quoted in Frank, *Einstein: His Life and Times*, p. 144

With fame I become more and more stupid, which of course is a very common phenomenon.

Letter to Heinrich Zangger, December 1919; Einstein Archive 39-726; also quoted in Dukas and Hoffmann, *Albert Einstein, the Human Side*, p. 8

Let me tell you what I look like: pale face, long hair, and a tiny beginning of a paunch. In addition, an awkward gait, and a cigar in the mouth . . . and a pen in pocket or hand. But crooked legs and warts he does not have, and so is quite handsome—also no hair on his hands as is so often found on ugly men. So it is indeed a pity that you did not see me.

Postcard to eight-year-old cousin Elisabeth Ney, September 1920; Einstein Archive 36-525; also quoted in Dukas and Hoffmann, *Albert Einstein, the Human Side*, p. 44

Just as the man in the fairy tale who turned whatever he touched into gold, with me everything becomes newspaper noise.

Letter to Max Born, September 9, 1920; Einstein Archive 8-151

Personally, I experience the greatest degree of pleasure in having contact with works of *art*. They furnish me with happy feelings of an intensity such as I cannot derive from other realms.

1920; quoted in Moszkowski, *Conversations with Einstein*, p. 184

It strikes me as unfair, and even in bad taste, to select a few individuals for boundless admiration, attributing superhuman powers of mind and character to them. This has been my fate, and the contrast between the popular estimate of my powers and achievements and the reality is simply grotesque.

From an interview for *Nieuwe Rotterdamsche Courant*, 1921; reprinted in *Ideas and Opinions*, pp. 3–7

If my theory of relativity is proven successful, Germany will claim me as a German and France will declare that I am a citizen of the world. Should my theory prove untrue, France will say that I am a German, and Germany will declare that I am a Jew.

From an address to the French Philosophical Society at the Sorbonne, April 6, 1922; see French press clipping, April 7, 1922, Einstein Archive 36-378; and *Berliner Tageblatt*, April 8, 1922, Einstein Archive 79-535

To punish me for my contempt for authority, Fate made me an authority myself.

Aphorism for a friend, September 18, 1930; Einstein Archive 36-598; also quoted in Hoffmann, *Albert Einstein: Creator and Rebel*, p. 24.

I am an artist's model.

October 31, 1930, to a passenger on a train who asked him his occupation, reflecting Einstein's feeling that he was constantly posing for sculptures and paintings; Einstein Archive 21-006; also quoted in ibid., p. 4

I have never looked upon ease and happiness as ends in themselves—such an ethical basis I call the ideal of a pigsty. . . . The ideals which have lighted my way, and time after time have given me new courage to face life cheerfully, have been Kindness, Beauty, and Truth.

From "What I Believe," in *Forum and Century* 84 (1930), pp. 193–194; reprinted in *Ideas and Opinions*, pp. 8–11

I am truly a "lone traveler" and have never belonged to my country, my home, my friends, or even my immediate family, with my whole heart. In the face of all this, I have never lost a sense of distance and the need for solitude.

Ibid.

A hundred times every day I remind myself that my inner and outer lives are based on the labors of other people, living and dead, and that I must exert myself in order to give in the same measure as I have received and am still receiving.

Ibid.

It is an irony of fate that I myself have been the recipient of excessive admiration and reverence from my fellow-beings, through no fault and no merit of my own.

Ibid.

Professor Einstein begs you to treat your publications for the time being as if he were already dead.

Written on Einstein's behalf by his secretary, Helen Dukas, March 1931, after he was besieged by one manuscript too many; Einstein Archive 46-487

Although I am a typical loner in my daily life, my consciousness of belonging to the invisible community of those who strive for truth, beauty, and justice has preserved me from feeling isolated.

From "My Credo," for the German League for Human Rights, 1932; quoted in Leach, *Living Philosphies*, p. 3

Although I try to be universal in thought, I am European by instinct and inclination.

Daily Express (London), September 11, 1933; quoted in Holton, *Advancement of Science*, p. 126

People flatter me so long as I don't get in their way. [Otherwise] they immediately turn to abuse and calumny in defense of their interests.

Letter to a pacifist friend, published in *Mein Weltbild*, 1934

I have acclimated extremely well here, live like a bear in its cave, and feel more at home than ever before in my eventful life. This bearlike quality has increased because of the death of my companion, who was more attached to people [than I].

Letter to Max Born, ca. 1937, after the death of Einstein's wife, Elsa; quoted in Born, *Einstein-Born Briefwechsel*, p. 177

I wouldn't want to live if I did not have my work. . . . In any case, it's good that I'm already old and personally don't have to reckon on a long future.

Letter to Michele Besso, October 10, 1938, reflecting on Hitler's rise to power; Einstein Archive 7-376

Why is it that nobody understands me, and everybody likes me?

From an interview, *New York Times*, March 12, 1944

I never worry about the future. It comes soon enough.

Aphorism, 1945–46; Einstein Archive 36-570

I have to apologize to you that I am still among the living. There *will* be a remedy for this, however.

Letter to a child, Tyffany Williams, August 25, 1946, after she expressed surprise that Einstein was still alive; Einstein Archive 42-612

There have already been published by the bucketfuls such brazen lies and utter fictions about me that I would long since have gone to my grave if I had let myself pay attention to them.

Letter to the writer Max Brod, February 22, 1949; Einstein Archive 34-066

My scientific work is motivated by an irresistible longing to understand the secrets of nature and by no other feelings. My love for justice and the striving to contribute toward the improvement of human conditions are quite independent from my scientific interests.

Letter to F. Lentz, August 20, 1949, in answer to a letter asking Einstein about his scientific motivation; Einstein Archive 58-418

It is a strange thing to be so widely known yet be so lonely. But it is a fact that this kind of popularity . . . is forcing its victim into a defensive position which leads to isolation.

Letter to E. Marangoni, October 1, 1952; Einstein Archive 60-406

I have no special talents. I am only passionately curious.

Letter to Carl Seelig, March 11, 1952; Einstein Archive 39-013

All my life I have dealt with objective matters; hence I lack both the natural aptitude and the experience to deal properly with people and to exercise official functions.

Statement to Abba Eban, November 18, 1952, turning down the presidency of Israel after Chaim Weizmann's death; Einstein Archive 28-943

In the past it never occurred to me that every casual remark of mine would be snatched up and recorded. Otherwise I would have crept further into my shell.

Letter to Carl Seelig, October 25, 1953; Einstein Archive 39-053

All manner of fable is being attached to my personality, and there is no end to the number of ingeniously devised tales. All the more do I appreciate and respect what is truly sincere.

Letter to Queen Elizabeth of Belgium, March 28, 1954; Einstein Archive 32-410

I'm not the kind of snob or exhibitionist that you take me to be and furthermore have nothing of value to say (of immediate concern) as you seem to assume.

In reply to a letter, May 1954, asking him to send a message to a new museum in Chile, to be put on display for others to admire; Einstein Archive 60-624

It is quite curious, even abnormal, that with your superficial knowledge about the subject you are so confident of your judgment. I regret that I cannot spare the time to occupy myself with dilettantes.

Letter to dentist G. Lebau, who claimed he had a better theory of relativity, July 10, 1954; the dentist returned Einstein's letter with a note written at the bottom: "I am thirty years old; it takes time to learn humility." Einstein Archive 60-226 and 60-227

If I were a young man again and had to decide how to make a living, I would not try to become a scientist or scholar or teacher. I would rather choose to be a plumber or a peddler, in the hope of finding that modest degree of independence still available under present circumstances.

To *The Reporter* magazine, November 18, 1954; also quoted in Nathan and Norden, *Einstein on Peace*, p. 613

Only in mathematics and physics was I, through self-study, far beyond the school curriculum, and also with regard to philosophy so far as it had to do with the school curriculum.

From a 1955 letter; quoted in Hoffmann, *Albert Einstein: Creator and Rebel*, p. 20

To me it is enough to wonder at the secrets.

Quoted in A&E Television Einstein Biography, VPI International, 1991

Arrows of hate have been shot at me too, but they have never hit me, because somehow they belonged to another world with which I have no connection whatsoever.

Quoted in *Out of My Later Years*, p. 13

My intuition was not strong enough in the field of mathematics to differentiate clearly the fundamentally important . . . from the rest of the more or less dispensable erudition. Also, my interest in the study of nature was no doubt stronger. . . . In this field I soon learned to scent out that which might lead to fundamentals and to turn aside . . . from the multitude of things that clutter up the mind and divert it from the essentials.

Quoted in Schilpp, *Autobiographical Notes*, p. 15

The only way to escape the corruption of praise is to go on working. . . . There is nothing else.

Quoted by Lincoln Barnett, "On His Centennial, the Spirit of Einstein Abides in Princeton," *Smithsonian*, February 1979, p. 74

God gave me the stubbornness of a mule and a fairly keen scent.

Quoted in Whitrow, *Einstein: The Man and His Achievement*, p. 91

When I was young, all I wanted and expected from life was to sit quietly in some corner doing my work without the public paying attention to me. And now see what has become of me.

Quoted in Hoffmann, *Albert Einstein: Creator and Rebel*, p. 4

When I examine myself and my methods of thought, I come close to the conclusion that the gift of fantasy [imagination] has meant more to me than my talent for absorbing absolute knowledge.

Recalled by a friend on the one hundredth anniversary of Einstein's birth, celebrated February 18, 1979; quoted in Ryan, *Einstein and the Humanities*, p. 125

I have never obtained any ethical values from my scientific work.

Quoted in Michelmore, *Einstein: Profile of the Man*, p. 251

That little word "we" I mistrust and here's why:
No man of another can say, "He is I."
Behind all agreement lies something amiss
All seeming accord cloaks a lurking abyss.

Verse quoted in Dukas and Hoffmann, *Albert Einstein, the Human Side*, p. 100

I have finished my task here.

Said as he was dying; Einstein Archive 39-095

On America and Americans

Taking the oath of U.S. allegiance, with Helen Dukas (*left*) and Margot Einstein, Trenton, New Jersey, 1940. (AIP Emilio Segré Visual Archives)

I am happy to be in Boston. I have heard of Boston as one of the most famous cities of the world and the center of education. I am happy to be here and expect to enjoy my visit to this city and Harvard.

On his visit to the city with Chaim Weizmann; *New York Times*, May 17, 1921; contributed by A. J. Kox of the Einstein Papers Project, Boston, in retaliation for the many quotations about Princeton in this book (see below)

If Americans are less scholarly than Germans, they have more enthusiasm and energy, which cause a wider spread of new ideas among the people.

New York Times, July 12, 1921

The smile on the faces of the people . . . is symbolical of one of the greatest assets of the American. He is friendly, self-confident, optimistic—and without envy.

From an interview for *Nieuwe Rotterdamsche Courant*, 1921; also quoted in *Berliner Tageblatt*, July 7, 1921; reprinted in *Ideas and Opinions*, pp. 3–7

The American lives even more for his goals, for the future, than the European. Life for him is always becoming, never being. . . . He is less of an individualist than the European . . . more emphasis is laid on the "we" than the "I."

Ibid.

I have warm admiration for American institutes of scientific research. We are unjust in attempting to ascribe the increasing superiority of American research work exclusively to superior wealth; devotion, patience, a spirit of comradeship, and a talent for cooperation play an important part in its success.

Ibid.

A firm approach is indispensable everywhere in America; otherwise one receives no pay and little esteem.

Letter to Maurice Solovine, January 14, 1922; Einstein Archive 21-157; published in *Letters to Solovine*, p. 49

Never have I experienced from the fair sex such energetic rejection of all my advances; or, if I have, never from so many at once.

Answer to an American women's organization, January 4, 1928, which had protested Einstein's visit to America; Einstein Archive 48-818; published in *Mein Weltbild*

America is today the hope of all honorable men who respect the rights of their fellow men and who believe in the principle of freedom and justice.

"Message for Germany," dictated over the telephone on December 7, 1941, to a White House correspondent; quoted in Nathan and Norden, *Einstein on Peace*, p. 320

The only justifiable purpose of political institutions is to assure the unhindered development of the individual. . . . That is why I consider myself particularly fortunate to be an American.

Ibid.

There is, however, a somber point in the social outlook of Americans. Their sense of equality and human dignity is mainly limited to men of white skin. . . . The more I feel an American, the more this situation pains me.

From an address at Lincoln University upon receipt of an honorary doctorate, May 1946; quoted in *Out of My Later Years*, under "The Negro Question," p. 127; see also "Blacks/Racism" under "Miscellaneous Subjects"

The separation [between Jews and Gentiles] is even more pronounced [in America] than it ever was anywhere in Western Europe, including Germany.

Letter to Hans Muehsam, March 24, 1948; Einstein Archive 38-371

I hardly ever have felt as alienated from people as I do right now. . . . The worst is that nowhere is there anything with which one can identify. Brutality and lies are everywhere.

Letter to Gertrud Warschauer, July 15, 1950, about the McCarthy era; Einstein Archive 39-505

The German calamity of years ago repeats itself: people acquiesce without resistance and align themselves with the forces of evil.

Letter to Queen Elizabeth of Belgium, January 6, 1951, about McCarthyism in America; Einstein Archive 32-400; also quoted in Nathan and Norden, *Einstein on Peace*, p. 554

I have become a kind of *enfant terrible* in my new homeland, due to my inability to keep silent and to swallow everything that happens here.

Letter to Queen Elizabeth of Belgium, March 28, 1954; Einstein Archive 32-410

ON HIS ADOPTED HOMETOWN OF PRINCETON, NEW JERSEY

I found Princeton fine. A pipe as yet unsmoked. Young and fresh.

New York Times, July 8, 1921

Princeton is a wonderful little spot, a quaint and ceremonious village of puny demigods on stilts. Yet, by ignoring certain social conventions, I have been able to create for myself an atmosphere conducive to study and free from distraction.

Letter to Queen Elizabeth of Belgium, November 20, 1933; Einstein Archive 32-369

My fame begins outside of Princeton. My word counts for little in Fine Hall.

On his lack of influence on decision-making on the Princeton campus, 1934–40? (The old Fine Hall is now Jones Hall, where the East Asian Studies department is located.) Quoted in Infeld, *Quest*, p. 302

Einstein in his study at his Princeton home, facing the university's Graduate Tower. (Lotte Jacobi Archives, University of New Hampshire)

I am very happy with my new home in this friendly country and with the liberal atmosphere of Princeton.

From an interview, "Peace Must Be Waged," for *Survey Graphic*, August 1934; quoted in Nathan and Norden, *Einstein on Peace*, p. 262

As an elderly man, I have remained estranged from the society here.

Letter to Queen Elizabeth of Belgium, February 16, 1935; Einstein Archive 32-385

I am privileged by fate to live here in Princeton as if on an island that . . . resembles the charming palace garden in Laeken. Into this small university town the chaotic voices of human strife barely penetrate. I am almost ashamed to be living in such peace while all the rest struggle and suffer.

Letter to Queen Elizabeth of Belgium, March 20, 1936; Einstein Archive 32-387

In the face of all the heavy burdens which I have borne in recent years, I feel doubly thankful that there has fallen to my lot in Princeton University a place for work and a scientific atmosphere which could not be better or more harmonious.

Letter to university president Harold Dodds, January 14, 1937; Einstein Archive 52-823

A banishment to paradise.

On going to Princeton, quoted in Sayen, *Einstein in America*, p. 64

You are surprised, aren't you, at the contrast between my fame throughout the world . . . and the isolation and quiet in which I live here? I wished for this isolation all my life, and now I have finally achieved it here in Princeton.

Quoted in Frank, *Einstein: His Life and Times*, p. 297

On Death

With friend Paul Ehrenfest, who later committed suicide. (Watercolor by M. Kamerlingh-Onnes. AIP Emilio Segré Visual Archives)

I have firmly decided to bite the dust with a minimum of medical assistance when my time comes, and up to then to sin to my wicked heart's content.

Letter to Elsa Einstein, August 11, 1913; *CPAE*, Vol. 5, Doc. 466

I feel myself so much a part of everything living that I am not in the least concerned with the beginning or ending of the concrete existence of any one person in this eternal flow.

Letter to Hedwig Born, wife of physicist Max Born, April 18, 1920; Einstein Archive 31-475; also quoted in Seelig, *Helle Zeit, Dunkle Zeit*, p. 36

I know what it is to see one's mother in the throes of death without being able to do anything about it. There is no consolation for it. We must all go through this, since it is a certain part of life.

Letter to Hedwig Born, June 18, 1920; Einstein Archive 8-257

Our death is not an end if we can live on in our children and the younger generation. For they are us; our bodies are only wilted leaves on the tree of life.

Letter to Dutch physicist Heike Kamerlingh-Onnes's widow, February 25, 1926; Einstein Archive 14-389

Neither on my deathbed nor before will I ask myself such a question. Nature is not an engineer or a contractor, and I myself am a part of Nature.

In answer to a question concerning what facts would determine if his life was a success or failure, November 12, 1930; Einstein Archive 45-751; also quoted in Dukas and Hoffmann, *Albert Einstein, the Human Side,* p. 92

I feel unable to participate in your projected TV broadcast "The Last Two Minutes." It seems to me not so relevant how people are to spend the last two minutes before their final deliverance.

In answer to a request that he take part in a television program on how some famous people would spend the last two minutes of their lives, August 26, 1950; Einstein Archive 60-684

I myself should also already be dead, but I am still here.

To E. Schaerer-Meyer, July 27, 1951; Einstein Archive 60-525

Look deep, deep into nature, and then you will understand everything better.

To Margot Einstein, after his sister Maja's death, 1951; quoted by Hanna Loewy in A&E Television Einstein Biography, VPI International, 1991

To one bent on age, death will come as a release. I feel this quite strongly now that I have grown old myself and have come to regard death like an old debt, at long last to be discharged. Still, instinctively one does everything possible to delay this last fulfillment. This is the game which Nature plays with us.

Letter to a friend, 1954 or 1955; quoted in Nathan and Norden, *Einstein on Peace*, p. 616

I want to go when *I* want. It is tasteless to prolong life artificially. I have done my share; it is time to go. I will do it elegantly.

Quoted by Helen Dukas in her letter to A. Pais, April 30, 1955; see Pais, *Subtle Is the Lord*, p. 477; also quoted in A&E Television Einstein Biography, VPI International, 1991

I want to be cremated so people won't come to worship at my bones.

Quoted by A. Pais, *Manchester Guardian*, December 17, 1994

On Education and Academic Freedom

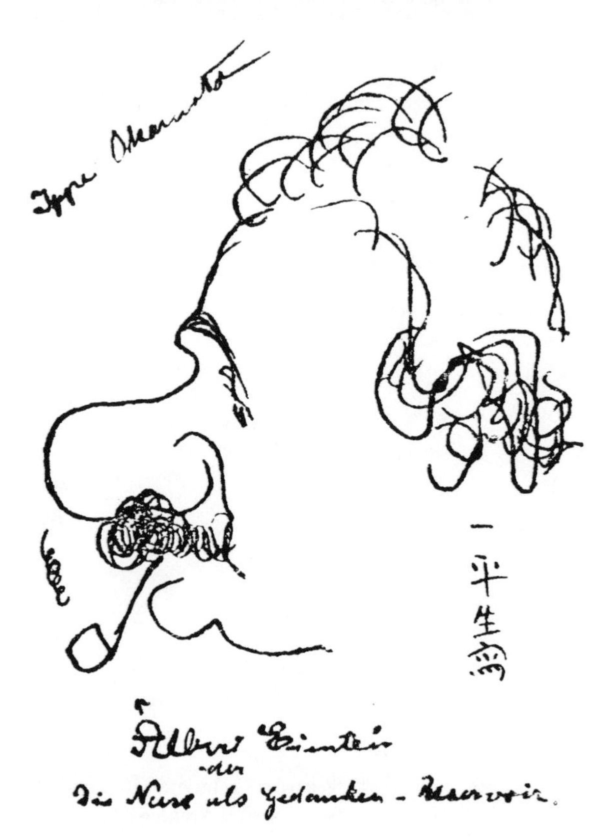

"The nose as thought reservoir." (Drawing by Ippei Okamoto. AIP Emilio Segré Visual Archives)

The inclination of the pupil for a particular profession must not be neglected, especially [because] such inclination usually asserts itself at an early age, being occasioned by personal gifts, by example of other members of the family, and by various other circumstances.

1920; quoted in Moszkowski, *Conversations with Einstein*, p. 65

Most teachers waste their time by asking questions which are intended to discover what a pupil does *not* know, whereas the true art of questioning has for its purpose to discover what the pupil knows or is capable of knowing.

Ibid.

It is not so very important for a person to learn facts. For that he does not really need a college. He can learn them from books. The value of an education in a liberal arts college is not the learning of many facts but the training of the mind to think something that cannot be learned from textbooks.

1921, on Thomas Edison's opinion that a college education is useless; quoted in Frank, *Einstein: His Life and Times*, p. 185

It would be better if you begin to teach others only after you yourself have learned something.

To Arthur Cohen, age 12, who submitted a paper to Einstein, December 26, 1928; Einstein Archive 25-044

Never regard your study as a duty, but as the enviable opportunity to learn to know the liberating influence of beauty in the realm of the spirit for your own personal joy and to the profit of the community to which your later work belongs.

In the Princeton freshman publication *The Dink,* December 1933; quoted in Don Oberdorfer, *Princeton: The First 250 Years* (Princeton University Press, 1995), p. 127

Humiliation and mental oppression by ignorant and selfish teachers wreak havoc in the youthful mind that can never be undone and often exert a baleful influence in later life.

Quoted in *Almanak van het Leidsche Studentencorps* (Doesburg-Verlag, Leiden, 1934)

To me the worst thing seems to be for a school principally to work with the methods of fear, force, and artificial authority. Such treatment destroys sound sentiments, the sincerity, and the self-confidence of the pupil. It produces the submissive subject.

From an address in Albany, New York, October 15, 1936; published as "On Education" in *Out of My Later Years*

The aim [of education] must be the training of independently acting and thinking individuals who, however, see in the service to the community their highest life achievement.

Ibid.

The school should always have as its aim that the young [person] leave it as a harmonious personality, not as a specialist.

Ibid.

Otherwise he—with his specialized knowledge—more closely resembles a well-trained dog than a harmoniously developed person.

New York Times, October 5, 1952

Freedom of teaching and of opinion in book or press is the foundation for the sound and natural development of any people.

At a gathering for Freedom of Opinion, 1936, quoted in *Einstein on Humanism*, p. 50

The crippling of individuals I consider the worst evil of capitalism. Our whole educational system suffers from this evil. An exaggerated competitive attitude is inculcated into the student, who is trained to worship acquisitive success as a preparation for his future career.

From "Why Socialism?" *Monthly Review*, May 1949

Teaching should be such that what is offered is perceived as a valuable gift and not as a hard duty.

New York Times, October 5, 1952

By academic freedom I understand the right to search for truth and to publish and teach what one holds to be true. This right implies also a duty: one must not conceal any part of what one has recognized to be true. It is evident that any restriction of academic freedom acts in such a way as to hamper the dissemination of knowledge among the people and thereby impedes national judgment and action.

Statement for a conference of the Emergency Civil Liberties Committee, March 13, 1954; quoted in Nathan and Norden, *Einstein on Peace*, p. 551

In the teaching of geography and history a sympathetic understanding [should] be fostered for the characteristics of the different peoples of the world, especially for those whom we are in the habit of describing as "primitive."

From an address delivered at the Conference of the Progressive Education Association, November 23, 1934, first published in *Einstein on Humanism*, p. 94

On Family

With sister Maja, 1884: "But where are its wheels?" (Courtesy of Lotte Jacobi Archives, University of New Hampshire)

ABOUT OR TO FIRST WIFE, MILEVA MARIĆ

According to Einstein, he was married to Mileva, who came from a Serbo-Greek peasant background, for seventeen years but never really knew her. Unbeknownst to Einstein at the time of marriage, schizophrenia occurred on Mileva's mother's side of the family, and she too was a depressed, untrusting person. She was also physically disfigured due to tuberculosis contracted in childhood, and this added to her emotional problems. Unable to accept their eventual divorce, she became bitter, causing difficulties in Einstein's relationship with his sons, to whom he tried to remain close, as evidenced by the many letters he wrote to Hans Albert. (See the forthcoming volume 8 of *CPAE* for these letters as well as letters to Mileva in which the couple tries to deal with its financial and parental difficulties after the separation.) These tragic circumstances, according to Einstein, left their mark on him into his old age and could account for his deep involvement in impersonal things. (See letters to Carl Seelig, March 26 and May 5, 1952; Einstein Archive 39-016 and 39-020)

Mama threw herself on the bed, buried her head in the pillow, and wept like a child. After regaining her composure, she immediately shifted to a desperate attack: "You are ruining your future and destroying your opportunities." "No decent family will have her." "If she gets pregnant you'll really be in a mess." With this outburst, which was preceded by many others, I finally lost my patience.

Letter to Mileva Marić, July 29, 1900, after telling his mother that he and Mileva planned to marry; they married January 6, 1903; *CPAE*, Vol. 1, Doc. 68

I long terribly for a letter from my beloved witch. I can hardly believe that we will be separated for so much longer—only now do I see how madly in love with you I am! Indulge yourself completely, so that you will become a radiant little darling and as wild as a street urchin.

Letter to Mileva Marić, August 1, 1900; *Love Letters*, p. 21; *CPAE*, Vol. 1, Doc. 69

How was I able to live alone before, my little everything? Without you I lack self-confidence, passion for work, and enjoyment of life—in short, without you, my life is no life.

Letter to Mileva Marić, August 14?, 1900; *Love Letters*, p. 26; *CPAE*, Vol. 1, Doc. 72

My parents are very worried about my love for you. . . . They weep for me almost as if I had died. Again and again they complain that I have brought misfortune upon myself by my devotion to you.

Letter to Mileva Marić, August–September 1900; *Love Letters*, p. 29; *CPAE*, Vol. 1, Doc. 74

Without the thought of you I would no longer want to live among this sorry herd of humans. But having you makes me proud, and your love makes me happy. I will be doubly happy when I can press you to my heart once again and see those loving eyes which shine for me alone, and kiss your sweet mouth which trembles blissfully for me alone.

Ibid.

I am also looking forward to working on our new studies. You must continue with your investigations—how proud I will be to have a little Ph.D. for a sweetheart while I remain a completely ordinary person!

Letter to Mileva Marić, September 13, 1900; *Love Letters*, p. 32; *CPAE*, Vol. 1, Doc. 75

Shall I look around for possible jobs for you [in Zurich]? I think I'll try to find some private lessons that I can later turn over to you. Or do you have something else in mind? . . . No matter what happens, we'll have the most wonderful life in the world.

Letter to Mileva Marić, September 19, 1900; *Love Letters*, p. 33; *CPAE*, Vol. 1, Doc. 76

I am so lucky to have found you—a creature who is my equal, and who is as strong and independent as I am!

Letter to Mileva Marić, October 3, 1900; *Love Letters*, p. 36; *CPAE*, Vol. 1, Doc. 79

You'll see for yourself how bright and cheerful I have become and how all my frowning is a thing of the past. And I love you so much again! It was only out of nervousness that I was so mean to you . . . and am longing so much to see you again.

Letter to Mileva Marić, April 30, 1901; *Love Letters*, p. 46; *CPAE*, Vol. 1, Doc. 102

If only I could give you some of my happiness so you would never be sad and pensive again.

Letter to Mileva Marić, May 9, 1901; *Love Letters* p. 51; *CPAE*, Vol. 1, Doc. 106

My wife goes [to Berlin] with very mixed feelings because she is afraid of the relatives, probably mostly you. . . . But you and I can very well be happy with each other without her having to be hurt. You cannot take away from her something she doesn't have.

Letter to newfound love, cousin Elsa Löwenthal, August 1913; *CPAE*, Vol. 5, Doc. 465

The situation in my house is ghostlier than ever: icy silence.

Letter to Elsa Löwenthal, October 16, 1913; *CPAE*, Vol. 5, Doc. 478

Do you think it's so easy to get a divorce if one doesn't have proof of the other party's guilt? . . . I treat my wife as an employee whom one cannot fire. I have my own bedroom and avoid being with her. . . . I don't know why you're so terribly upset by that. I'm absolutely my own master . . . as well as my own wife.

Letter to Elsa Löwenthal, before December 2, 1913; *CPAE*, Vol. 5, Doc. 488

[My wife, Mileva] is an unfriendly, humorless creature who gets nothing out of life and who, by her mere presence, extinguishes other people's joy of living.

Letter to Elsa Löwenthal, after December 2, 1913; *CPAE*, Vol. 5, Doc. 489

My wife whines incessantly to me about Berlin and her fear of the relatives. . . . My mother is good-natured, but she is a really fiendish mother-in-law. When she stays with us, the air is full of dynamite. . . . But both are to be blamed for the miserable relationship. . . . No wonder that the love of science thrives under these circumstances: it lifts me impersonally . . . from the vale of tears into peaceful spheres.

Letter to Elsa Löwenthal, after December 21, 1913; *CPAE*, Vol. 5, Doc. 497

I do not want to lose the children and I do not want them to lose me. . . . After all that has happened, a comradely relationship with you is out of the question. It shall be a loyal and businesslike relationship. All personal things must be kept to a minimum. . . . I don't expect to ask you for a divorce but only want that you stay in Switzerland with the children . . . and send me news of my beloved boys every two weeks. . . . In return, I assure you of proper comportment on my part, such as I would exercise toward any woman as a stranger.

Letter to Mileva Einstein-Marić, ca. July 18, 1914, on his offer to continue their marriage after his move to Berlin, to which she did not agree; Einstein Archive 75-854; *CPAE*, Vol. 8 (forthcoming), Doc. 22; also quoted in Highfield and Carter, *The Private Lives*, p. 170

She never reconciled herself to the separation and divorce, and a disposition developed reminiscent of the classical example of Medea. This darkened the relations with my two boys, to whom I was attached with tenderness. This tragic aspect of my life continued undiminished until my advanced age.

On wife Mileva, in letter to Carl Seelig, May 5, 1952; Einstein Archive 39-020

ABOUT OR TO SECOND WIFE, ELSA LÖWENTHAL

Einstein began a long-distance affair with his cousin Elsa, who lived in Berlin, in 1912, while he was still married to Mileva and living in Zurich. The affair continued after the family moved to Berlin in 1914. He was not divorced from Mileva, who soon returned to Zurich, until February 1919. In June he married Elsa, though for many years he had been telling friends that he did not intend to marry her. (See *CPAE*, Vol. 8, forthcoming)

I will always destroy your letters, as is your wish. I have already destroyed the first one.

Letter to Elsa Löwenthal, April 30, 1912, responding to her misgivings about their affair; *CPAE*, Vol. 5, Doc. 389

First wife, Mileva Marić, ca. 1896. (Courtesy of Schweizerische Landesbibliothek)

Pauline Koch Einstein, Albert's mother. (Courtesy of The Hebrew University of Jerusalem)

With second wife, Elsa Löwenthal, and stepdaughter Margot at home in Berlin, 1929. (Ullstein Bilderdienst, Berlin)

I suffer even more than you because you suffer only for what you do *not* have.

Letter to Elsa Löwenthal, May 7, 1912, alluding to his difficult wife, Mileva; *CPAE*, Vol. 5, Doc. 391

I am writing so late because I have misgivings about our affair. I have the feeling that it will not be good for us, nor for the others, if we form a closer attachment.

Letter to Elsa Löwenthal, May 21, 1912; *CPAE*, Vol. 5, Doc. 399

I now have someone of whom I can think with unrestrained pleasure and for whom I can live. . . . We will have each other, something we have missed so terribly, and will give each other the gift of equilibrium and a happy view of the world.

Letter to Elsa Löwenthal, October 10, 1913; *CPAE*, Vol. 5, Doc. 476

If you were to recite for me the most beautiful poem . . . my pleasure would not even approach the pleasure I felt when I received the mushrooms and goose cracklings you prepared for me; . . . you will surely not despise the primitive side of my nature that is revealed by this.

Letter to Elsa Löwenthal, November 7, 1913; *CPAE*, Vol. 5, Doc. 482

ABOUT OR TO HIS CHILDREN

Einstein had two sons, Hans Albert and Eduard, and a daughter, referred to as "Lieserl," from his first marriage, and two stepdaughters, Ilse and Margot, from his second marriage. Only Hans Albert had children. Eduard was mentally ill and lived in Switzerland, and Einstein's only contact with him after leaving Europe in 1933 was through his biographer, Carl Seelig; he told Seelig he never wrote to Eduard for reasons he could not fully analyze himself (Einstein Archive 39-060). Lieserl was born in January 1902 before he and Mileva were married and was presumably given up for adoption or died of the effects of scarlet fever; no mention is made of her after September 1903. (See *CPAE*, Vol. 5, and *Love Letters*)

I'm very sorry about what has befallen Lieserl. It's so easy to suffer lasting effects from scarlet fever. If only this will pass. As what is the child registered? We must take precautions that problems don't arise for her later.

Letter to Mileva Marić, September 19, 1903; *Love Letters*, p. 78

It is a thousand pities for the boy that he must pass his life without hope of a normal existence. Since the insulin injections have proved unsuccessful, I have no further hopes from the medical side. I think it better on the whole to let Nature run its course.

Letter to Michele Besso, November 11, 1940, about son Eduard; Einstein Archive 7-378

It is a joy for me to have a son who has inherited the main trait of my personality: the ability to rise above mere existence by sacrificing oneself through the years for an impersonal goal. This is the best, indeed the only way in which we can make ourselves independent from personal fate and from other human beings.

Letter to Hans Albert, May 1, 1954; quoted in Highfield and Carter, *The Private Lives*, p. 258

Unfortunately, I have to admit that I didn't think about it, but your wife reminded me.

Letter to Hans Albert on his fiftieth birthday, May 1954; quoted in an interview with Bernard Mayer, in Whitrow, *Einstein*, p. 21

When Margot speaks, you see flowers growing.

Commenting on his stepdaughter's love of nature; quoted by Frieda Bucky in "You Have to Ask Forgiveness," *The Jewish Quarterly* 15, no. 4 (Winter 1967–68), p. 33

ABOUT SISTER MAJA AND MOTHER PAULINE

Yes, but where are its wheels?

> Two-year-old Albert, after the birth of Maja in 1881, upon being told he would now have something to play with; in "Biographical Sketch" by Maja Winteler-Einstein, in *CPAE*, Vol. 1, p. lvii

My mother and sister seem somewhat petty and philistine to me, despite the sympathy I feel for them. It is interesting how gradually life changes us in the very subtleties of our soul, so that even the closest of family ties dwindle into habitual friendship. Deep inside we no longer understand one another and are incapable of empathizing with the other, or knowing what emotions move the other.

> Letter to Mileva Marić, early August 1899; *Love Letters*, p. 9; *CPAE*, Vol. 1, Doc. 50

My mother has died. . . . We are all completely exhausted. . . . One feels in one's bones the significance of blood ties.

> Letter to Heinrich Zangger, early March 1920; Einstein Archive 39-732

On Friends, Specific Scientists, and Others

With Niels Bohr. (Photo by Paul Ehrenfest. AIP Emilio Segré Visual Archives)

ON MICHELE BESSO

Now he has departed from this strange world a little ahead of me. That signifies nothing. For us believing physicists the distinction between past, present, and future is only a stubbornly persistent illusion.

On lifelong friend Michele Besso, in letter of condolence to Besso family, March 21, 1955, less than a month before his own death; Einstein Archive 7-245

What I admired most in him as a human being is that he managed to live for so many years not only in peace but also in lasting harmony with a woman—an undertaking in which I twice failed rather disgracefully.

Ibid.

ON NIELS BOHR

Not often in my life has a human being caused me such joy by his mere presence as you have done.

Letter to Niels Bohr, May 2, 1920; Einstein Archive 8-065

Bohr was here, and I'm as much in love with him as you are. He is like an extremely sensitive child who moves around in this world in sort of a trance.

Letter to Paul Ehrenfest, May 4, 1920; Einstein Archive 9-486

He is truly a man of genius. . . . I have full confidence in his way of thinking.

Letter to Paul Ehrenfest, March 23, 1922; Einstein Archive 10-035

He utters his opinions like one who perpetually gropes and never like one who believes to possess the definitive truth.

Letter to Bill Becker, March 20, 1954; Einstein Archive 8-109

ON LOUIS BRANDEIS

I know of no other person who combines such profound intellectual gifts with such self-renunciation while finding the whole meaning of his life in quiet service to the community.

Letter to Supreme Court Justice Louis Brandeis, November 10, 1936; Einstein Archive 35-046

ON MARIE CURIE

I do not believe Mme Curie is power-hungry or hungry for whatever. She is an unpretentious, honest person with more than her share of responsibilities and burdens. She has a sparkling intelligence, but despite her passionate nature she is not attractive enough to represent a danger to anyone.

Letter to Heinrich Zangger, November 7, 1911, regarding Curie's alleged affair with married French physicist Paul Langevin; *CPAE*, Vol. 5, Doc. 303

I am deeply grateful to you and your friends that you so cordially allowed me to participate in your daily life. To witness such marvelous camaraderies of such people is the most uplifting thing I can think of. Everything looked so natural and uncomplicated with you, like a good work of art. . . . I wish to ask your forgiveness if by any chance my rough manners sometimes made you feel uncomfortable.

Letter to Marie Curie, April 3, 1913; *CPAE*, Vol. 5, Doc. 435

Madame Curie is very intelligent but as cold as a herring, meaning that she is lacking in all feelings of joy and sorrow. Almost the only way in which she expresses her feelings is to rail at things she doesn't like. And she has a daughter who is even worse—like a grenadier. This daughter is also very gifted.

Letter to Elsa Löwenthal, August 11?, 1913; *CPAE*, Vol. 5, Doc. 465

Her strength, her purity of will, her austerity toward herself, her objectivity, her incorruptible judgment—all these were of a kind seldom found joined in a single individual. . . . Once she had recognized a certain way as the right one, she pursued it without compromise and with extreme tenacity.

At Curie memorial celebration, Roerich Museum, New York, November 23, 1935; Einstein Archive 5-142

ON PAUL EHRENFEST

His sense of inadequacy, objectively unjustified, plagued him incessantly, often robbing him of the peace of mind necessary for tranquil research. . . . His tragedy lay precisely in an almost morbid lack of self-confidence. . . . The strongest relationship in his life was that to his wife and fellow worker . . . his intellectual equal. . . . He repaid her with a veneration and love such as I have not often witnessed in my life.

After physicist and close friend Paul Ehrenfest's suicide; quoted in *Almanak van het Leidsche Studentencorps* (Doesburg-Verlag, Leiden, 1934)

ON MICHAEL FARADAY

This man loved mysterious Nature as a lover loves his distant beloved.

Letter to Gertrud Warschauer, December 27, 1952; Einstein Archive 39-517

ON SIGMUND FREUD

The old one . . . had a sharp vision; no illusions lulled him to sleep except for an often exaggerated faith in his own ideas.

Letter to A. Bacharach, July 25, 1949; Einstein Archive 57-629

ON GALILEO

Alas, you find [vanity] in so many scientists. It has always hurt me that Galileo did not acknowledge the work of Kepler.

To I. Bernard Cohen, April 1955; quoted in French, *Einstein: A Centenary Volume,* p. 41

ON GANDHI

A leader of his people, unsupported by any outward authority: a politician whose success rests not upon craft nor the mastery of technical devices, but simply on the convincing power of his personality; a victorious fighter who has always scorned the use of force; a man of wisdom and humility, armed with resolve and inflexible consistency, who has devoted all his strength to the uplifting of his people and the betterment of their lot; a man who has confronted the brutality of Europe with the dignity of the simple human being, and thus at all times risen superior.

Generations to come, it may be, will scarce believe that such a one as this ever in flesh and blood walked upon this earth.

Statement on occasion of Gandhi's seventieth birthday, 1939; unpublished elsewhere, quoted in *Einstein on Humanism*, p. 94

I believe that Gandhi held the most enlightened views of all the political men in our time. We should strive to do things in his spirit; not to use violence in fighting for our cause and to refrain from taking part in anything we believe is evil.

New York Times, June 19, 1950; also quoted in Pais, *Einstein Lived Here*, p. 110

Gandhi, the greatest political genius of our time . . . gave proof of what sacrifice man is capable once he has discovered the right path.

Letter to Asian Congress for World Federation, November 1952; quoted in Nathan and Norden, *Einstein on Peace*, p. 584

Gandhi's development resulted from extraordinary intellectual and moral forces in combination with political ingenuity and a unique situation.

1953; ibid., p. 594

ON GOETHE

I feel in him a certain condescending attitude toward the reader, a certain lack of humble devotion which, especially in great men, has such a comforting effect.

Letter to L. Caspar, April 9, 1932; Einstein Archive 49-380

ON HITLER

A man with limited intellectual abilities and unfit for any useful work, bursting with envy and bitterness against all whom circumstance and nature had favored over him. . . . He picked up human flotsam on the street and in the taverns and organized them around himself.

From an unpublished manuscript, 1935; quoted in Nathan and Norden, *Einstein on Peace*, pp. 263–264

ON HEIKE KAMERLINGH-ONNES

A life has ended which will always remain a role model for future generations. . . . No other person have I known for whom duty and joy were one and the same. This was the reason for his harmonious life.

Letter to the Dutch physicist's widow, February 25, 1926; Einstein Archive 14-389

ON KANT

What appears to me the most important thing in Kant's philosophy is that it speaks of a priori concepts for the construction of science.

At a discussion in the Société Française de Philosophie, July 1922; in *Bulletin Société Française de Philosophie* 22 (1922), p. 91; reprinted in *Nature* 112 (1923), p. 253

ON KEPLER

Kepler was one of the few who are simply incapable of doing anything but stand up openly for their convictions in every field. . . . [His] lifework was possible only once he succeeded in freeing himself to a great extent from the intellectual traditions into which he was born. . . . He does not speak of it, but the inner struggle is reflected in his letters.

From preface to *Johannes Kepler: Life and Letters*, ed. Carola Baumgardt (New York: Philosophical Library, 1951)

ON PAUL LANGEVIN

If he loves Mme Curie and she loves him, they do not have to run off together, because they have plenty of opportunities to meet in Paris. But I did not at all get the impression that something special exists between the two of them; rather, I found all three of them bound by a pleasant and innocent relationship.

Letter to Heinrich Zangger, November 7, 1911, on the French physicist's rumored affair with Marie Curie; *CPAE*, Vol. 5, Doc. 303

There are so few in any generation in whom clear insight into the nature of things is joined with an intense feeling for the challenge of true humanity and the capacity for militant action. When such a man departs, he leaves a gap that seems unbearable to his survivors. . . . His desire to promote the happier life for all men was perhaps even stronger than his craving for pure intellectual enlightenment. No one who appealed to his social conscience ever went away emptyhanded.

Quoted in *La Pensée*, February–March 1947

I had already heard of Langevin's death. He was one of my dearest acquaintances, a true saint, and talented besides. It is true that the politicians exploited his goodness, for he was unable to see through the base motives that were so foreign to his nature.

Letter to Maurice Solovine, April 9, 1947; Einstein Archive 21-250; also quoted in *Letters to Solovine*, p. 99

ON LENIN AND ENGELS

Outside Russia, Lenin and Engels are of course not valued as scientific thinkers and no one might be interested to refute them as such. The same might also be the case in Russia, except there one doesn't dare say so.

Letter to K. R. Leistner, September 8, 1932; Einstein Archive 50-877

ON H. A. LORENTZ

Lorentz is a marvel of intelligence and exquisite tact. A living work of art! In my opinion he was the most intelligent of the theoreticians present [at the Solvay Congress in Brussels].

Letter to Heinrich Zangger, November 1911, on the Dutch physicist, whom Einstein loved and admired; *CPAE*, Vol. 5, Doc. 305

My feeling of intellectual inferiority with regard to you cannot spoil the great delight of [our] conversations, especially because the fatherly kindness you show to all people does not allow any feeling of despondency to arise.

Letter to Lorentz, February 18, 1912; *CPAE*, Vol. 5, Doc. 360

He shaped his life like an exquisite work of art down to the smallest detail. His never-failing kindness and generosity and his sense of justice, coupled with a sure and intuitive understanding of people and human affairs, made him a leader in any sphere he entered.

Address at the grave of H. A. Lorentz, 1928; published in *Mein Weltbild*

People do not realize how great was the influence of Lorentz on the development of physics. We cannot imagine how it would have gone had not Lorentz made so many great contributions.

Quoted by Robert Shankland in French, *Einstein: A Centenary Volume*, p. 39

ON ERNST MACH

In him the immediate pleasure gained in seeing and comprehending—Spinoza's *amor dei intellectualis*—was so strong that he looked at the world with the curious eyes of a child until well into old age, so that he could find joy and contentment in understanding how everything is connected.

Obituary for the philosopher whose critique of Newton played a role in Einstein's development of general relativity theory, even though Mach himself was critical of the theory; in *Physikalische Zeitschrift*, April 1, 1916; *CPAE*, Vol. 6, Doc. 29

Mach was as good a scholar of mechanics as he was a deplorable philosopher.

Quoted in *Bulletin Société Française de Philosophie* 22 (1922), p. 91; reprinted in *Nature* 112 (1923), p. 253; see also *CPAE*, Vol. 6, Doc. 29, n. 6

ON ALBERT A. MICHELSON

I always think of Michelson as the artist in science. His greatest joy seemed to come from the beauty of the experiment itself and the elegance of the method employed.

Letter to Robert Shankland, September 17, 1953, on the physicist who experimentally helped confirm Einstein's special theory of relativity; Einstein Archive 17-203

ON NEWTON

His great and lucid ideas will retain their unique significance for all time as the foundation of our whole modern conceptual structure in the sphere of natural philosophy.

Statement in *The Times* (London), November 28, 1919

In my opinion, the greatest creative geniuses are Galileo and Newton, whom I regard in a certain sense as forming a unity. And in this unity Newton is [the one] who has achieved the most imposing feat in the realm of science.

> 1920; quoted in Moszkowski, *Conversations with Einstein*, p. 40

In one person he combined the experimenter, the theorist, the mechanic, and, not least, the artist in exposition.

> From the "Introduction" to Newton, *Opticks* (McGraw-Hill, 1932)

Newton . . . you found just about the only way possible in your age for a man of the highest reasoning and creative powers. The concepts you created are even today still guiding our thinking in physics, although we now know they will have to be replaced . . . if we aim at a profounder understanding of relationships.

> Quoted in Schilpp, *Albert Einstein: Philosopher-Scientist*, p. 31

Newton was the first to succeed in finding a clearly formulated basis from which he could deduce a wide field of phenomena by means of mathematical thinking—logically, quantitatively, and in harmony with experience.

Manchester Guardian, Christmas 1942

ON EMMY NOETHER

On receiving the new work from Fräulein Noether, I again find it a great injustice that she cannot lecture officially. I would be very much in favor of taking energetic steps in the ministry [to overturn this rule].

Letter to Felix Klein, December 27, 1918, on the brilliant mathematician who was not allowed to be on the faculty of the University of Göttingen because she was a woman; Einstein Archive 14-459

It would not have done the Old Guard at Göttingen any harm, had they picked up a thing or two from her. She certainly knows what she is doing.

Postcard to David Hilbert, May 24, 1918; Einstein Archive 13-125

In the judgment of the most competent living mathematicians, Fräulein Noether was the most significant creative mathematical genius this far produced since the higher education of women began.

Letter to the *New York Times* upon the death of Emmy Noether, May 4, 1935

ON MAX PLANCK

How different, and how much better it would be for mankind if there were more like him. . . . It seems that fine characters in every age and continent must remain apart from the world, unable to influence events.

Letter to Frau Planck, November 10, 1947, on her husband, the German physicist; Einstein Archive 19-406

He was one of the finest people I have ever known . . . but he really didn't understand physics, [because] during the eclipse of 1919 he stayed up all night to see if it would confirm the bending of light by the gravitational field. If he had really understood [the general theory of relativity], he would have gone to bed the way I did.

Quoted by Ernst Straus in French, *Einstein: A Centenary Volume*, p. 31

ON FRANKLIN D. ROOSEVELT

No matter when this man might have left us, we would have felt that we had suffered an irreplaceable loss. . . . May he have a lasting influence on the hearts and minds of men!

Statement upon the president's death, in *Aufbau* (New York), April 27, 1945. (According to the *New York Times*, August 19, 1946, Einstein was sure that FDR would have forbidden the atomic bombing of Hiroshima had he been alive. Einstein had written a letter to FDR in March 1945 warning him of the bomb's devastating effects; the president died before he had a chance to read it.)

I'm so sorry that Roosevelt is president—otherwise I would visit him more often.

To friend Frieda Bucky; quoted in *The Jewish Quarterly* 15, no. 4 (Winter 1967–68), p. 34

ON BERTRAND RUSSELL

The clarity, certainty, and impartiality you apply to the logical, philosophical, and human issues in your books are unparalleled in our generation.

Letter to Russell, October 14, 1931; Einstein Archive 33-155, 75-544; also quoted in Grüning, *Ein Haus für Albert Einstein*, p. 369

Great spirits have always encountered violent opposition from mediocre minds. The mediocre mind is incapable of understanding the man who refuses to bow blindly to conventional prejudices and chooses instead to express his opinions courageously and honestly.

On controversy surrounding Russell's appointment to the faculty of the City University of New York; quoted in the *New York Times*, March 13, 1940

ON ALBERT SCHWEITZER

He is the only Westerner who has had a moral effect on this generation comparable to Gandhi's. As in the case of Gandhi, the extent of this effect is overwhelmingly due to the example he gave by his own life's work.

Unpublished statement, 1953, originally intended for Einstein's 1934 book, *Mein Weltbild*; quoted in Sayen, *Einstein in America*, p. 296

ON SPINOZA

Spinoza is one of the most profound and pure people that our Jewish race has produced.

In a letter of 1946, quoted in Dürrenmatt, *Albert Einstein: Ein Vortrag*, p. 22

ON TOLSTOI

He remains in many ways the foremost prophet of our time.... There is no one today with Tolstoi's deep insight and moral force.

From an interview, "Peace Must Be Waged," for *Survey Graphic*, August 1934; quoted in Nathan and Norden, *Einstein on Peace*, p. 261

ON CHAIM WEIZMANN

The chosen one of the chosen people.

Letter to Weizmann, October 27, 1923; Einstein Archive 33-366

On Germans and Germany

Einstein receiving the Planck Medal from Max Planck, Berlin, July 1929. (AIP Emilio Segré Visual Archives)

Berlin is the place to which I am most closely bound by human and scientific ties.

Letter to K. Haenisch, Prussian Minister of Education, September 8, 1920; Einstein Archive 36-022; quoted in Frank, *Einstein: His Life and Times*, p. 169; also quoted in the *New York Times*, November 21, 1920, p. 10

Germany had the misfortune of becoming poisoned, first because of plenty and then because of want.

Aphorism, 1923; Einstein Archive 36-591

The statements I have issued to the Press were concerned with my intention to resign my position in the Academy and renounce my Prussian citizenship; I gave as my reason for these steps that I did not wish to live in a country where the individual does not enjoy equality before the law and freedom to say and teach what he likes.

Letter to the Prussian Academy of Sciences, April 5, 1933; Einstein Archive 29-295

You have also remarked that a "good word" on my part for "the German people" would have produced a great effect abroad. To this I must reply that such testimony as you suggest would have been equivalent to a repudiation of all those notions of justice and liberty for which I have all my life stood. Such a testimony would not be, as you put it, a good word for the German nation.

Reply to the Prussian Academy of Sciences, April 12, 1933, after it accepted Einstein's resignation; Einstein Archive 29-297

I cannot understand the passive response of the whole civilized world to this modern barbarism. Doesn't the world see that Hitler is aiming for war?

October 1, 1933; quoted by a reporter for *Bunte Welt* (Vienna); quoted in Pais, *Einstein Lived Here*, p. 194

The overemphasized military mentality in the German State was alien to me even as a boy. When my father moved to Italy he took steps, at my request, to have me released from German citizenship because I wanted to become a Swiss citizen.

1933; quoted in Hoffmann, *Albert Einstein: Creator and Rebel*, p. 26

Germany the way it used to be was [a cultural] oasis in the desert.

Letter to Alfred Kerr, July 1934; Einstein Archive 50-687

For centuries . . . the Germans have been trained in hard work and were made to learn many things, but they have also been trained in slavish submission, military routine, and brutality.

From an unpublished manuscript, 1935; quoted in Nathan and Norden, *Einstein on Peace*, p. 263

They have always had the tendency to treat psychopaths like knights. But they have never been able to accomplish it so successfully as at the present time.

Written as a scribble on the reverse of a letter dated July 28, 1939; Einstein Archive 53-160

Due to their wretched traditions the Germans are so messed up that it will be very difficult to remedy the situation by sensible, not to say humane, means. I hope that by the end of the war . . . they will largely kill each other off.

Letter to Otto Juliusburger, Summer 1942; Einstein Archive 38-199; also quoted in Sayen, *Einstein in America*, p. 146

The Germans as an entire people are responsible for these mass murders and must be punished as a people. . . . Behind the Nazi party stand the German people who elected Hitler after he had in his book and in his speeches made his shameful intentions clear beyond the possibility of misunderstanding.

On the heroes of the Warsaw Ghetto, in *Bulletin of the Society of Polish Jews* (New York), 1944

After the Germans massacred my Jewish brothers in Europe, I will have nothing further to do with Germans. . . . It is otherwise with those few who remained firm within the range of the possible.

Letter to Arnold Sommerfeld, December 14, 1946; Einstein Archive 21-368 (Einstein included Otto Hahn, Max von Laue, Max Planck, and Arnold Sommerfeld among the few)

The crime of the Germans is truly the most abominable ever to be recorded in the history of the so-called civilized nations. The conduct of the German intellectuals—seen as a group—was no better than that of the mob.

Letter to Otto Hahn, January 28, 1949; Einstein Archive 12-072

On Humankind

EINSTEIN SIMPLIFIED
s. harris

Children don't heed the life experiences of their parents, and nations ignore history. Bad lessons always have to be learned anew.

Aphorism, October 12, 1923; Einstein Archive 36-589

It is people who make me seasick—not the sea. But I'm afraid that science is yet to find a solution for this ailment.

Letter to Herr Schering-Kahlbaum, November 28, 1930; Einstein Archive 36-531

Enjoying the joys of others and suffering with them—these are the best guides for man.

Letter to Valentine Bulgakov, November 4, 1931; Einstein Archive 45-702

The true value of a human being is determined primarily by how he has attained liberation from the self.

June 1932; Einstein Archive 60-492; published in *Mein Weltbild*

One can't teach a cat not to catch birds.

Letter to Florence Schneller, March 9, 1936; Einstein Archive 51-756

Common convictions and aims, similar interests, will in every society produce groups that, in a certain sense, act as units. There will always be friction between such groups—the same sort of aversion and rivalry that exists between individuals. . . . In my opinion, uniformity in a population would not be desirable, even if it were attainable.

From "Why Do They Hate the Jews?" *Collier's* magazine, November 26, 1938

It is better for people to be like the beasts . . . they should be more intuitive; they should not be too conscious of what they are doing while they are doing it.

From a conversation recorded by Algernon Black, Fall 1940; Einstein Archive 54-834

We have to do the best we can. This is our sacred human responsibility.

Ibid.

There is only one road to true human greatness: through the school of hard knocks.

Comment on W. White's article, "Why I Remain a Negro," October 1947; Einstein Archive 59-009

We all are nourished and housed by the work of our fellowmen and we have to pay honestly for it not only by work chosen for the sake of our inner satisfaction but by work which, according to general opinion, serves them. Otherwise one becomes a parasite, however modest our needs might be.

Letter to a man who wanted to spend his time being subsidized to study rather than to work, July 28, 1953; Einstein Archive 59-180

To obtain an assured favorable response from people, it is better to offer them something for their stomachs rather than their brains.

Letter to a chocolate manufacturer, March 19, 1954; Einstein Archive 60-401

Fear or stupidity has always been the basis of most human actions.

Letter to E. Mulder, April 1954; Einstein Archive 60-609

On Jews, Israel, Judaism, and Zionism

With Israeli prime minister David Ben-Gurion, Princeton, 1951. (AIP Emilio Segré Visual Archives)

I am not at all eager to go to America but am doing it only in the interest of the Zionists, who must beg for dollars to build educational institutions in Jerusalem and for whom I act as high priest and decoy. . . . But I do what I can to help those in my tribe who are treated so badly everywhere.

Letter to Maurice Solovine, March 8, 1921; published in *Letters to Solovine*, p. 41

Where dull-witted clansmen of our tribe were praying aloud, their faces turned to the wall, their bodies swaying to and fro. A pathetic sight of men with a past but without a present.

On his visit to the Wailing Wall in Jerusalem, February 3, 1923, recorded in his travel diary; Einstein Archive 29-129 to 29-131

Should we be unable to find a way to honest cooperation and honest pacts with the Arabs, then we have learned absolutely nothing during our 2,000 years of suffering and deserve all that will come to us.

Letter to Chaim Weizmann, November 25, 1929; Einstein Archive 33-411

Jewry has proved that the intellect is the best weapon in history. . . . It is the duty of us Jews to put at the disposal of the world our several-thousand-years-old sorrowful experience and, true to the ethical traditions of our forefathers, become soldiers in the fight for peace, united with the noblest elements in all cultural and religious circles.

From an address at a Jewish meeting in Berlin, 1929; quoted in Frank, *Einstein: His Life and Times,* p. 156

The Jewish religion is . . . a way of sublimating everyday existence. . . . It demands no act of faith—in the popular sense of the term—on the part of its members. And for that reason there has never been a conflict between our religious outlook and the world outlook of science.

In *Forum* 83 (1930), p. 373

I have always been annoyed by the undignified assimilationist cravings and strivings which I have observed in so many of my [Jewish] friends. . . . These and similar happenings have awakened in me the Jewish national sentiment.

1931, in *About Zionism,* p. 40

Judaism is not a creed: the Jewish God is simply a negation of superstition, an imaginary result of its elimination. It is also an attempt to base the moral law on fear, a regrettable and discreditable attempt. Yet it seems to me that the strong moral tradition of the Jewish nation has to a large extent shaken itself free from this fear. It is clear also that "serving God" was equated with "serving the living." The best of the Jewish people, especially the Prophets and Jesus, contended tirelessly for this.

Published in *Mein Weltbild*, 1934; reprinted in *Ideas and Opinions*, pp. 185–187

The pursuit of knowledge for its own sake, an almost fanatical love of justice and the desire for personal independence—these are the features of the Jewish tradition which makes me thank my stars that I belong to it.

Ibid.

There are no German Jews, there are no Russian Jews, there are no American Jews. Their only difference is their daily language. There are in fact only Jews.

From a speech at a Purim dinner at the German-Jewish Club in New York, March 24, 1935; quoted in *Aufbau* (New York), March 16, 1979; see also *Einstein: The Human Side*, p. 61, for an explanation

The intellectual decline brought on by shallow materialism is a far greater menace to the survival of the Jew than the numerous external foes who threaten his existence with violence.

New York Times, June 8, 1936

I should much rather see reasonable agreement with the Arabs on the basis of living together in peace than the creation of a Jewish state.

From a speech entitled "Our Debt to Zionism," before the National Labor Committee for Palestine on April 17, 1938, in New York; full text in *New Palestine* (Washington, D.C.), April 28, 1938

Judaism owes a great debt of gratitude to Zionism. The Zionist movement has revived among Jews the sense of community. It has performed productive work . . . in Palestine, to which self-sacrificing Jews throughout the world have contributed. . . . In particular, it has been possible to lead a not inconsiderable part of our youth toward a life of joyous and creative work.

Ibid.

My awareness of the essential nature of Judaism resists the idea of a Jewish state with borders, an army, and a measure of temporal power. . . . I am afraid of the inner damage Judaism will sustain—especially from the development of a narrow nationalism within our ranks, which we have already had to fight strongly even without a Jewish state. . . . A return to a nation in the political sense of the word would be equivalent to turning away from the spiritualization of our community which we owe to the genius of our prophets.

Ibid.

The Jews as a group may be powerless, but the sum of the achievements of their individual members is everywhere considerable and telling, even though those achievements were made in the face of obstacles.

"Why Do They Hate the Jews?" *Collier's* magazine, November 26, 1938

[The Nazis] see the Jews as a nonassimilable element that cannot be driven into uncritical acceptance and that . . . threatens their authority because of its insistence on popular enlightenment of the masses.

Ibid.

The Jew who abandons his faith (in the formal sense of the word) is in a position similar to a snail that abandons its shell. He remains a Jew.

Ibid.

The bond that has united the Jews for thousands of years and that unites them today is, above all, the democratic ideal of social justice, coupled with the ideal of mutual aid and tolerance among all men. . . . The second characteristic of Jewish tradition is the high regard in which it holds every form of intellectual aspiration and spiritual effort.

Ibid.

[Zionism is] nationalism whose aim is not power but dignity.

Excerpt from an article in the *New York Times Magazine*, March 12, 1944; Einstein Archive 29-102

Zionism gave the German Jews no great protection against annihilation. But it did give the survivors the inner strength to endure the debacle with dignity and without losing their healthy self-respect.

To an anti-Zionist Jew, January 1946?; quoted in Dukas and Hoffmann, *Albert Einstein, the Human Side*, p. 65

The wisdom and moderation the leaders of the new state have shown gives me confidence that gradually relations will be established with the Arab people which are based on fruitful cooperation and mutual respect and trust. For this is the only means through which both peoples can attain true independence from the outside world.

Statement to the Hebrew University of Jerusalem upon receipt of an honorary doctorate, March 15, 1949; Einstein Archive 28-854, 37-296

This University is today a living thing, a home of free learning and teaching and happy brotherly work. There it is, on the soil that our people have liberated under great hardships; there it is, a spiritual center of a flourishing and buoyant community whose accomplishments have finally met with the universal recognition they deserve.

Ibid.

The Jews of Palestine did not fight for political independence for its own sake, but they fought to achieve free immigration for the Jews of many countries where their very existence was in danger; free immigration also for all those who were longing for a life among their own. It is no exaggeration to say that they fought to make possible a sacrifice perhaps unique in history.

From an NBC radio broadcast for the United Jewish Appeal Conference, Atlantic City, November 27, 1949; Einstein Archive 58-904

The support for cultural life is of primary concern to the Jewish people. We would not be in existence today as a people without this continued activity in learning.

Statement on the occasion of the twenty-fifth anniversary of the Hebrew University of Jerusalem; quoted in the *New York Times*, May 11, 1950

My relationship to the Jewish people has become my strongest human bond, ever since I became fully aware of our precarious situation among the nations of the world.

Statement to Abba Eban, November 18, 1952; Einstein Archive 28-943

For the young State to achieve real independence, and conserve it, there must be a group of intellectuals and experts produced in the country itself.

Quoted in the *New York Times*, May 25, 1953

Israel is the only place on earth where Jews have the possibility to shape public life according to their own traditional ideals.

Address at a planning conference of American Friends of the Hebrew University, in Princeton, N.J., September 19, 1954; Einstein Archive 28-1054

The attitude we adopt toward the Arab minority will provide the real test of our moral standards as a people.

Quoted in Nathan and Norden, *Einstein on Peace*, p. 638

Only when we [Jews] have the courage to regard ourselves as a nation, only when we have respect for ourselves, can we win the respect of others.

Quoted in Hoffmann, "Einstein and Zionism," p. 237

The heart says yes, but the mind says no.

Response to an invitation to accept a position at the Hebrew University of Jerusalem; ibid., p. 241

Zionism indeed represents a new Jewish ideal that we can restore to the Jewish people their joy in existence.

Quoted in Dukas and Hoffmann, *Albert Einstein, the Human Side*, p. 63

If I were to be president, sometimes I would have to say to the Israeli people things they would not like to hear.

> To Margot Einstein, on his decision to turn down the presidency of Israel; quoted in Sayen, *Einstein in America*, p. 247

On Life

Caricature by George Schreiber, 1935. (University of Texas at Austin, Humanities Research Center)

If there is no price to be paid, it is also not of value.

Aphorism, June 20, 1927; Einstein Archive 36-582

I believe that a simple and unassuming life is good for everybody, physically and mentally.

From "What I Believe," in *Forum and Century* 84 (1930), pp. 193–194; reprinted in *Ideas and Opinions*, pp. 8–11

Only a life lived for others is a life worthwhile.

In answer to a question asked by the editors of *Youth*, a journal of Young Israel of Williamsburg, N.Y.; quoted in the *New York Times*, June 20, 1932; Einstein Archive 60-492

Strange is our situation here upon the earth. Each of us comes for a short visit, not knowing why, yet sometimes seeming to divine a purpose.

From "My Credo," for the German League of Human Rights, 1932; also quoted in Leach, *Living Philosophies*, p. 3

The life of the individual has meaning only insofar as it aids in making the life of every living thing nobler and more beautiful. Life is sacred, that is to say, it is the supreme value, to which all other values are subordinate.

From "Is There a Jewish Point of View?" published in *Mein Weltbild*, 1934; reprinted in *Ideas and Opinions*, pp. 185–187

When the expected course of everyday life is interrupted, we realize that we are like shipwrecked people trying to keep their balance on a miserable plank in the open sea, having forgotten where they came from and not knowing whither they are drifting.

Letter to a couple who unexpectedly lost a child or grandchild, April 26, 1945; Einstein Archive 56-852

We must try to recognize what in our accepted tradition is damaging to our fate and dignity—and shape our lives accordingly.

On the American attitude toward blacks, from an address at Lincoln University upon receipt of an honorary doctorate; *New York Times*, May 4, 1946, p. 7; also quoted in *Out of My Later Years* under "The Negro Question," p. 128

The most precious things in life are not those one gets for money.

Aphorism, 1946; Einstein Archive 36-576

A life directed chiefly toward the fulfillment of personal desires sooner or later always leads to bitter disappointment.

Letter to L. Lee, January 16, 1954; Einstein Archive 60-235

Every reminiscence is colored by today's being what it is, and therefore by a deceptive point of view.

Quoted in Schilpp, *Albert Einstein: Philosopher-Scientist*, p. 3

If you want to live a happy life, tie it to a goal, not to people or things.

Quoted by Ernst Straus, in French, *Einstein: A Centenary Volume*, p. 32

On Pacifism

SECOND NEWS SECTION

For News, Subscriptions or Advertising Call ATlantic 6100.

SATURDAY MORNING,

Pittsburgh Post-Gazette

DECEMBER 29, 1934.

SPORTS, FINANCIAL, CLASSIFIED SECTION

WORLD OURS

Constantly Expressive—Einstein Warms Up to His Subject

ATOM ENERGY HOPE IS SPIKED BY EINSTEIN

Efforts at Loosing Vast Force Is Called Fruitless.

SAVANT TALKS HERE

Now Indicates Doubt Of Relativity Theory He Made Famous.

Front page of the *Pittsburgh Post-Gazette*, December 29, 1934. (AIP Emilio Segré Visual Archives)

Einstein was a pacifist from his youth until 1933, when Hitler forced his hand on the issue. From 1933 to 1945, he saw some need for military action under certain circumstances, but he felt that a "supranational" world government was necessary to preserve civilization and individual freedoms. From 1945 until his death in 1955, he spoke out in favor of world government as a moral imperative and in support of the control of nuclear weapons.

He who cherishes the values of culture cannot fail to be a pacifist.

From a handbook on pacifism, *Die Friedensbewegung*, 1922; quoted in Nathan and Norden, *Einstein on Peace*, p. 55; quoted as "A human being who considers spiritual values as supreme must be a pacifist" in Clark, *Einstein*, p. 428

In all cases where a reasonable solution of difficulties is possible, I favor honest cooperation and, if this is not possible under prevailing circumstances, Gandhi's method of peaceful resistance to evil.

From ibid.; quoted in Nathan and Norden, *Einstein on Peace*, p. 596

The conscientious objector is a revolutionary. In deciding to disobey the law he sacrifices his personal interests to the most important cause of working for the betterment of society.

From ibid.; quoted in Nathan and Norden, *Einstein on Peace*, pp. 542–543

My pacifism is an instinctive feeling, a feeling that possesses me because the murder of people is disgusting. My attitude is not derived from any intellectual theory but is based on my deepest antipathy to every kind of cruelty and hatred.

To Paul Hutchinson, editor of *Christian Century*, July 1929; quoted in Nathan and Norden, *Einstein on Peace*, p. 98; also quoted in Clark, *Einstein*, p. 427

I have made no secret, either privately or publicly, of any sense of outrage over officially enforced military and war service. I regard it as a duty of conscience to fight against such barbarous enslavement of the individual with every means available.

Statement to the Danish newspaper *Politiken*, August 5, 1930

That a man can take pleasure in marching in formation to the strains of a band is enough to make me despise him.

From "What I Believe," in *Forum and Century* 84 (1930), pp. 193–194; reprinted in *Ideas and Opinions*, pp. 8–11

I believe serious progress [in the abolition of war] can be achieved only when men become organized on an international scale and refuse, as a body, to enter military or war service.

Statement in *Jugendtribüne*, April 17, 1931

There are two ways of resisting war: the legal way and the revolutionary way. The legal way involves the offer of alternative service not as a privilege for a few but as a right for all. The revolutionary view involves an uncompromising resistance, with a view to breaking the power of militarism in time of peace or the resources of the state in time of war.

Statement in *The New World*, July 1931

I appeal to all men and women, whether they be eminent or humble, to declare that they will refuse to give any further assistance to war or the preparation of war.

In a statement to the War Resisters International, Lyons, 1931; quoted in Frank, *Einstein: His Life and Times*, p. 158; also quoted in the *New York Times*, August 2, 1931

I believe the most important mission of the state is to protect the individual and make it possible for him to develop into a creative personality. . . . The state violates this principle when it compels us to do military service.

From *The Nation* 33 (1931), p. 300; also quoted in the *New York Times*, November 22, 1931; published in *Mein Weltbild*

I am not only a pacifist but a militant pacifist. I am willing to fight for peace. . . . Is it not better for a man to die for a cause in which he believes, such as peace, than to suffer for a cause in which he does not believe, such as war?

From an interview on a visit to the United States, 1931; quoted in Alfred Lief, ed., *The Fight against War* (New York: John Day, 1933)

It is my belief that the problem of bringing peace to the world on a supranational basis will be solved only by employing Gandhi's method on a larger scale.

Letter to G. Nellhaus, March 20, 1951; Einstein Archive 60-683; also quoted in Nathan and Norden, *Einstein on Peace*, p. 543

I can identify my views nearly completely with those of Gandhi. But I would (individually and collectively) resist with violence an attempt to kill me or take away from me or my people the basic means of subsistence.

Letter to A. Morrisett, March 21, 1952; Einstein Archive 60-595

The goal of pacifism is possible only through a supranational organization. To stand unconditionally for this cause is . . . the criterion of true pacifism.

Ibid.

The more a country makes military weapons, the more insecure it becomes: if you have weapons, you become a target for attack.

From a conversation with M. Aram, January 1953; Einstein Archive 59-109

I am a *dedicated* but not an *absolute* pacifist; this means that I am opposed to the use of force under any circumstances except when confronted by an enemy who pursues the destruction of life as an *end in itself*.

Letter to a Japanese correspondent, June 23, 1953; Einstein Archive 61-297, 61-298

On Peace, War, the Bomb, and the Military

With Robert Oppenheimer. (International Communication Agency. AIP Emilio Segré Visual Archives)

That worst outcrop of herd life, the military system, which I abhor . . . this plague-spot of civilization ought to be abolished with all possible speed. Heroism on command, senseless violence, and all the loathsome nonsense that goes by the name of patriotism—how passionately I hate them! How vile and despicable seems war to me! I would rather be hacked into pieces than take part in such an abominable business.

From "What I Believe," in *Forum and Century* 84 (1930), pp. 193–194; reprinted in *Ideas and Opinions*, pp. 8–11

War is not a parlor game in which the players obediently stick to the rules. Where life and death are at stake, rules and obligations go by the board. Only the absolute repudiation of all war can be of any use here.

From an address to a group of German pacifist students, about 1930; published in *Mein Weltbild*; reprinted in *Ideas and Opinions*, p. 94

We must . . . dedicate our lives to drying up the source of war: ammunition factories.

Interview, May 23, 1932; published in *Pictorial Review*, February 1933; quoted in Clark, *Einstein*, p. 453

This is the problem: Is there any way of delivering mankind from the menace of war? It is common knowledge that with the advance of modern science, this issue has come to mean a matter of life and death for civilization as we know it; nevertheless, for all the zeal displayed, every attempt at its solution has ended in a lamentable breakdown.

Letter to Sigmund Freud, July 30, 1932; published by the International Institute for Cultural Cooperation, with Freud's reply; Einstein Archive 32-543; also quoted in Nathan and Norden, *Einstein on Peace*, p. 188

Anybody who really wants to abolish war must resolutely declare himself in favor of his own country's resigning a portion of its sovereignty in place of international institutions.

From "America and the Disarmament Conference of 1932"; published in *Mein Weltbild*, 1934; reprinted in *Ideas and Opinions*, p. 101

As long as armies exist, any serious conflict will lead to war. A pacifism which does not actively fight against the armament of nations is and must remain impotent.

Published in *Mein Weltbild*, 1934; reprinted in *Ideas and Opinions*, p. 111

[The likelihood of transforming matter into energy] is something akin to shooting birds in the dark in a country where there are only a few birds.

Remark at a 1935 press conference, three years before the atom was successfully split to cause fission; quoted in Nathan and Norden, *Einstein on Peace*, p. 290

It is unworthy of a great nation to stand idly by while small countries of great culture are being destroyed with a cynical contempt for justice.

From a message to a peace meeting, April 5, 1938; ibid., p. 279

Some recent work by E. Fermi and L. Szilard, which has been communicated to me in manuscript, leads me to expect that the element uranium may be turned into a new and important source of energy in the immediate future. Certain aspects of the situation which has arisen seem to call for watchfulness and, if necessary, quick action on the part of the Administration.

From a letter to President Franklin D. Roosevelt, August 2, 1939, resulting in the appropriation of government funds for the development of the atomic bomb; the letter was composed by Leo Szilard and signed by Einstein; Einstein Archive 33-088; full text reprinted in Clark, *Einstein*, pp. 556–557

This new phenomenon [atomic energy] would also lead to the construction of bombs. . . . A single bomb of this type, carried by boat and exploded in a port, might very well destroy the whole port, together with some of the surrounding territory. However, such bombs might prove to be too heavy for transportation by air.

Ibid.

Organized power can be opposed only by organized power. Much as I regret this, there is no other way.

Letter to a pacifist student, July 14, 1941; quoted in Nathan and Norden, *Einstein on Peace*, p. 319

I have done no work on [the atomic bomb], no work at all.

Quoted in the *New York Times*, August 12, 1945

As long as nations demand unrestricted sovereignty we shall undoubtedly be faced with still bigger wars, fought with bigger and technologically more advanced weapons.

Letter to Robert Hutchins, September 10, 1945; quoted in Nathan and Norden, *Einstein on Peace*, p. 337

The release of atomic energy has not created a new problem. It has merely made more urgent the necessity of solving an existing one.

From "Atomic War or Peace," *Atlantic Monthly,* November 1945

I do not believe that civilization will be wiped out in a war fought with the atomic bomb. Perhaps two-thirds of the people on earth would be killed, but enough men capable of thinking, and enough books, would be left to start out again, and civilization could be restored.

Ibid.

The secret of the bomb should be committed to a world government. . . . Do I fear the tyranny of a world government? Of course I do. But I fear still more the coming of another war or wars. Any government is certain to be evil to some extent. But a world government is preferable to the far greater evil of wars.

Ibid.

I do not consider myself the father of the release of atomic energy. My part in it was quite indirect. I did not, in fact, foresee that it would be released in my time. I believed only that it was theoretically possible. It became practical only through the accidental discovery of chain reaction, and this was not something I could have predicted.

Ibid.

It should not be forgotten that the atomic bomb was made in this country as a preventive measure; it was to head off its use by the Germans if they discovered it.

Ibid.

I am not saying the U.S. should not manufacture and stockpile the bomb, for I believe that it must do so; it must be able to deter another nation from making an atomic attack when it also has the bomb.

Ibid.

Since I do not foresee that atomic energy is to be a great boon for a long time, I have to say that for the present it is a menace. Perhaps it is well that it should be. It may intimidate the human race into bringing order into its international affairs, which, without the pressure of fear, it would not do.

Ibid.

The war is won, but the peace is not.

> Statement at the fifth Nobel Anniversary Dinner in New York; quoted in the *New York Times*, December 11, 1945; reprinted in *Ideas and Opinions*, pp. 115–117

Noncooperation in military matters should be an essential moral principle for all true scientists . . . who are engaged in basic research.

> January 20, 1947; quoted in Nathan and Norden, *Einstein on Peace*, p. 401

It is characteristic of the military mentality that nonhuman factors (atom bombs, strategic bases, weapons of all sorts, the possession of raw materials, etc.) are held essential, while the human being, his desires and thoughts—in short, the psychological factors—are considered as unimportant and secondary. . . . The individual is degraded . . . to "human materiel."

> From "The Military Mentality," *American Scholar*, Summer 1947

As long as there will be man, there will be wars.

> Letter to Philippe Halsmann, 1947; Einstein Archive 58-260 to 58-262

Where belief in the omnipotence of physical force gets the upper hand in political life, this force takes on a life of its own and proves stronger than the men who think to use force as a tool.

From an address in New York on receiving the One World award, April 27, 1948; published in *Out of My Later Years*

We scientists, whose tragic destiny it has been to help make the methods of annihilation ever more gruesome and more effective, must consider it our solemn and transcendent duty to do all in our power to prevent these weapons from being used for the brutal purpose for which they were invented.

Quoted in the *New York Times*, August 29, 1948

Responsibility lies with those who make use of these new tools and not with those who contribute to the progress of knowledge: therefore, with the politicians, not with the scientists.

From an interview by student Milton James, February 1949; Einstein Archive 58-014

So long as security is sought through national armament, no country is likely to renounce any weapon that seems to promise it victory in the event of war. In my opinion, security can be attained only by renouncing all national military defense.

Letter to Jacques Hadamard, December 29, 1949; Einstein Archive 12-064

If it [the effort to produce a hydrogen bomb] is successful, radioactive poisoning of the atmosphere and hence annihilation of any life on earth will have been brought within the range of what is technically possible.

From a contribution to Eleanor Roosevelt's television program on the implications of the H-bomb, February 13, 1950; reprinted in *Ideas and Opinions*, pp. 159–161

To my mind, to kill in war is not a whit better than to commit ordinary murder.

Quoted in the Japanese magazine *Kaizo*, Autumn 1952

The first atomic bomb destroyed more than the city of Hiroshima. It also exploded our inherited, outdated political ideas.

A co-signed statement quoted in the *New York Times*, June 12, 1953

There was never even the slightest indication of any potential technological application.

> Letter to Jules Isaac, February 28, 1955, refuting the idea that his special theory of relativity was responsible for atomic fission and the atom bomb (atomic fission, accomplished in December 1938 in Berlin by Otto Hahn and Fritz Strassmann, was made possible by the discovery of the neutron in 1932 by James Chadwick; fission requires neutrons); quoted in Nathan and Norden, *Einstein on Peace*, p. 623

There lies before us, if we choose, continued progress in happiness, knowledge, and wisdom. Shall we, instead, choose death, because we cannot forget our quarrels? We appeal, as human beings, to human beings: Remember your humanity and forget the rest.

> Einstein's last signed statement, issued with Bertrand Russell, April 11, 1955, one week before Einstein's death; Einstein Archive 33-212

Had I known that the Germans would not succeed in producing an atomic bomb, I never would have lifted a finger.

> Quoted in Vallentin, *Das Drama Albert Einsteins*, p. 278

The unleashing of power of the atom has changed everything but our modes of thinking and thus we drift toward unparalleled catastrophes.

Quoted in the *New York Times Magazine*, August 2, 1964

I made one mistake in my life—when I signed that letter to President Roosevelt advocating that the atomic bomb should be built. But perhaps I can be forgiven for that because we all felt that there was a high probability that the Germans were working on this problem and they might succeed and use the atomic bomb to become the master race.

Letter to Linus Pauling, recorded in Pauling's diary and recalled in the A&E Television Einstein Biography, VPI International, 1991; also quoted by Ted Morgan in *FDR* (New York: Simon and Schuster, 1985)

On Politics, Patriotism, and Government

At microphones, ca. 1950. (New York Times Paris Bureau. Courtesy National Archives)

Nationalism is an infantile disease. It is the measles of mankind.

Statement to G. S. Viereck, 1921; quoted in Dukas and Hoffmann, *Albert Einstein, the Human Side,* p. 38

My political ideal is that of democracy. Let every man be respected as an individual and no man idolized.

From "What I Believe," *Forum and Century* 84 (1930), pp. 193–194; reprinted in *Ideas and Opinions,* pp. 8–11

The state is made for man, not man for the state. . . . That is to say, the state should be our servant and not we its slaves.

In *The Nation* 33 (1931), p. 300; published in *Mein Weltbild*

As long as I have a choice, I will stay only in a country where political liberty, toleration, and equality of all citizens before the law are the rule. . . . These conditions do not obtain in Germany at the present time.

From "Manifesto," March 1933; published in *Mein Weltbild*; reprinted in *Ideas and Opinions*, p. 205

Nationalism, in my opinion, is nothing more than an idealistic rationalization for militarism and aggression.

From the first draft of a speech at Royal Albert Hall, London, October 3, 1933; quoted in Nathan and Norden, *Einstein on Peace*, p. 242

Politics is a pendulum whose swings between anarchy and tyranny are fueled by perennially rejuvenated illusions.

Aphorism, 1937; quoted in Dukas and Hoffmann, *Albert Einstein, the Human Side*, p. 38

There are times when the climate of the world is good for ethical things. Sometimes men trust one another and create good. At other times it is not so.

From a conversation recorded by Algernon Black, Fall 1940; Einstein Archive 54-834

When people live in a time of maladjustment, when there is tension and disequilibrium, they become unbalanced themselves and then may follow an unbalanced leader.

Ibid.

The greatest weakness of the democracies is economic fear.

Ibid.

The only salvation for civilization and the human race lies in the creation of a world government, with the security of nations founded upon law.

New York Times, September 15, 1945

Everything that is done in international affairs must be done from the following viewpoint: Will it help or hinder the establishment of world government?

From the text of a broadcast interview with P. A. Schilpp and F. Parmelee, May 29, 1946; Einstein Archive 29-105; see also Nathan and Norden, *Einstein on Peace*, p. 381

A world government must be created which is able to solve conflicts between nations by judicial decision. . . . This government must be based on a clear-cut constitution which is approved by the governments and the nations, and which has the sole disposition of offensive weapons.

New York Times, May 30, 1946; quoted in Pais, *Einstein Lived Here*, p. 232

We must learn the difficult lesson that the future of mankind will only be tolerable when our course, in world affairs as in all other matters, is based upon justice and law rather than the threat of naked power.

From a message for the Gandhi memorial service, February 11, 1948; quoted in Nathan and Norden, *Einstein on Peace*, p. 467

There is only *one* path to peace and security: the path of a supranational organization. One-sided armament on a national basis only heightens the general uncertainty and confusion without being an effective protection.

From an address in New York on receiving the One World award, April 27, 1948; published in *Out of My Later Years*

I advocate world government because I am convinced that there is no other possible way of eliminating the most terrible danger in which man has ever found himself. The objective of avoiding total destruction must have priority over any other objective.

Reply to a Soviet scientist's open letter in the *New York Times*, 1948; quoted in *Einstein on Humanism*, p. 45

To act intelligently in human affairs is only possible if an attempt is made to understand the thoughts, motives, and apprehensions of one's opponent so fully that one can see the world through his eyes.

Ibid., p. 39

Considerable economic security at the expense of liberty and political rights.

Describing communism, October 7, 1948, in answer to a question posed by Milton James; Einstein Archive 58-015

If the idea of world government is not realistic, then there is only *one* realistic view of our future: wholesale destruction of man by man.

Comment about the film *Where Will You Hide?* 1948; Einstein Archive 28-817

I have never been a Communist. But if I were I would not be ashamed of it.

Letter to Lydia B. Hewes, July 10, 1950; Einstein Archive 59-984

Mankind can be saved only if a supranational system, based on law, is created to eliminate the methods of brute force.

Statement in *Impact* 1 (1950), p. 104

Every intellectual who is called before one of the committees ought to refuse to testify; i.e., he must be prepared for jail and economic ruin . . . in the interest of the cultural welfare of his country.

Letter to William Frauenglass, May 16, 1953, on the McCarthy hearings; Einstein Archive 41-112

There is no such [anti-Communist] hysteria in the West European countries and there is no danger of their governments being overthrown by force or subversion, despite the fact that Communist parties are not persecuted or even ostracized.

Letter to E. Lindsay, July 18, 1953; Einstein Archive 60-326

Eastern Europe would never have become prey to Russia if the Western powers would have prevented German aggressive fascism under Hitler, which grave mistake made it necessary afterwards to beg Russia for help.

Ibid.

Party membership is a thing for which no citizen is obligated to give an accounting.

Letter to C. Lamont, January 2, 1954; Einstein Archive 60-178

The fear of communism has led to practices which have become incomprehensible to the rest of civilized mankind and expose our country to ridicule.

Message to Decalogue Society of Lawyers on receiving their merit award; *New York Times*, February 21, 1954

The current [House Un-American Activities Committee] investigations are an incomparably greater danger to our society than those few Communists in the country ever could be. These investigations have already undermined to a considerable extent the democratic character of our society.

Letter to Felix Arnold, March 19, 1954; Einstein Archive 59-118

In Plato's time, and even later, in Jefferson's time, it was still possible to reconcile democracy with a moral and intellectual aristocracy, while today democracy is based on a different principle—namely, that the other fellow is not better than I am. . . . This attitude doesn't altogether facilitate imitation.

On democracy and anti-intellectualism, in Niccolo Tucci's *New Yorker* profile, November 22, 1954, p. 54

Political passions, aroused everywhere, demand their victims.

Final written words, in an unpublished manuscript, April 12–14?, 1955; quoted in Pais, *Subtle Is the Lord*, p. 530

That is simple, my friend: because politics is more difficult than physics.

When asked why people could discover atoms but not the means to control them; recalled in the *New York Times*, April 22, 1955

In my opinion it is not right to bring politics into scientific matters, nor should individuals be held responsible for the government of the country to which they happen to belong.

To H. A. Lorentz, quoted in French, *Einstein: A Centenary Volume*, p. 187

One must divide one's time between politics and equations. But our equations are much more important to me.

Quoted by C. P. Snow in French, *Einstein: A Centenary Volume*, p. 8

On Religion, God, and Philosophy

In old age, early 1950s. (AIP Emilio Segré Visual Archives, Lande Collection)

Einstein's "religion," as he often explained it, was an attitude of cosmic awe and wonder and a devout humility before the harmony of nature, rather than a belief in a personal God who is able to control the lives of individuals.

Why do you write to me, "God should punish the English"? I have no close connection to either one or the other. I see only with deep regret that God punishes so many of His children for their numerous stupidities, for which only He Himself can be held responsible; in my opinion, only His nonexistence could excuse Him.

Letter to Edgar Meyer, a Swiss colleague, January 2, 1915; contributed by Robert Schulmann; also in *CPAE*, Vol. 8 (forthcoming)

In every true searcher of Nature there is a kind of religious reverence, for he finds it impossible to imagine that he is the first to have thought out the exceedingly delicate threads that connect his perceptions.

1920; quoted in Moszkowski, *Conversations with Einstein*, p. 46

Since our inner experiences consist of reproductions and combinations of sensory impressions, the concept of a soul without a body seems to me to be empty and devoid of meaning.

Letter to a Viennese woman, February 5, 1921; Einstein Archive 43-847; also quoted in Dukas and Hoffmann, *Albert Einstein, the Human Side*, p. 40

I cannot conceive of a personal God who would directly influence the actions of individuals. . . . My religiosity consists in a humble admiration of the infinitely superior spirit that reveals itself in the little that we . . . can comprehend of reality.

Letter to a banker in Colorado, August 1927; Einstein Archive 48-380; also quoted in Dukas and Hoffmann, *Albert Einstein, the Human Side*, p. 66

Everything is determined . . . by forces over which we have no control. It is determined for the insect as well as for the star. Human beings, vegetables, or cosmic dust—we all dance to a mysterious tune, intoned in the distance by an invisible piper.

In the *Saturday Evening Post*, October 26, 1929; quoted in Clark, *Einstein*, pp. 346–347

I believe in Spinoza's God who reveals himself in the harmony of all that exists, but not in a God who concerns himself with the fate and actions of human beings.

Telegram to a Jewish newspaper, 1929; Einstein Archive 33-272 (Spinoza reasoned that God and the material world are indistinguishable; the better one understands how the universe works, the closer one comes to God)

The man who is thoroughly convinced of the universal operation of the law of causation cannot for a moment entertain the idea of a being who interferes in the course of events. . . . He has no use for the religion of fear and equally little for social or moral religion. A God who rewards and punishes is inconceivable to him for the simple reason that a man's actions are determined by necessity, external and internal, so that in God's eyes he cannot be responsible, any more than an inanimate object is responsible for the motions it undergoes. . . . A man's ethical behavior should be based effectually on sympathy, education, and social ties and needs; no religious basis is necessary. Man would indeed be in a poor way if he had to be restrained by fear of punishment and hope of reward after death.

From "Religion and Science," *New York Times Magazine*, November 9, 1930, pp. 1–4; in German in *Berliner Tageblatt*, November 11, 1930

Everything that the human race has done and thought is concerned with the satisfaction of deeply felt needs and the assuagement of pain. One has to keep this constantly in mind if one wishes to understand spiritual movements and their development. Feeling and longing are the motive forces behind all human endeavor and human creations.

Ibid.

It is very difficult to elucidate this [cosmic religious] feeling to anyone who is entirely without it. . . . The religious geniuses of all ages have been distinguished by this kind of religious feeling, which knows no dogma and no God conceived in man's image; so that there can be no church whose central teachings are based on it. . . . In my view, it is the most important function of art and science to awaken this feeling and keep it alive in those who are receptive to it.

On "cosmic religion," a worship of the beauties and harmony of physics that became the common faith of physicists; ibid.

I maintain that the cosmic religious feeling is the strongest and noblest motive for scientific research.

Ibid.

I am of the opinion that all the finer speculations in the realm of science spring from a deep religious feeling. . . . I also believe that this kind of religiousness . . . is the only creative religious activity of our time.

In *Forum* 83 (1930), p. 373

I cannot conceive of a God who rewards and punishes his creatures, or has a will of the kind that we experience in ourselves. Neither can I nor would I want to conceive of an individual who survives his physical death; let feeble souls, from fear or absurd egoism, cherish such thoughts.

From "What I Believe," *Forum and Century* 84 (1930), pp. 193–194; reprinted in *Ideas and Opinions*, pp. 8–11

Our actions should be based on the ever-present awareness that human beings in their thinking, feeling, and acting are not free but are just as causally bound as the stars in their motion.

Statement to the Spinoza Society of America, September 22, 1932; Einstein Archive 33-291

Philosophy is like a mother who gave birth to and endowed all the other sciences. Therefore one should not scorn her in her nakedness and poverty, but should hope, rather, that part of her Don Quixote ideal will live on in her children so that they do not sink into philistinism.

Letter to Bruno Winawer, September 8, 1932; Einstein Archive 36-532; quoted in Dukas and Hoffmann, *Albert Einstein, the Human Side*, p. 106

I cannot imagine a God who rewards and punishes the objects of his creation, whose purposes are modeled after our own—a God, in short, who is but a reflection of human frailty. . . . It is enough for me to contemplate the mystery of conscious life perpetuating itself through all eternity, to reflect upon the marvelous structure of the universe which we can dimly perceive and to try humbly to comprehend even an infinitesimal part of the intelligence manifested in Nature.

From "My Credo," for the German League of Human Rights, 1932; quoted in Leach, *Living Philosophies*, p. 3

Organized religion may regain some of the respect it lost in the last war if it dedicates itself to mobilizing the goodwill and energy of its followers against the rising tide of illiberalism.

New York Times, April 30, 1934; also quoted in Pais, *Einstein Lived Here*, p. 205

You will hardly find one among the profounder sort of scientific minds without a religious feeling of his own. But it is different from the religiosity of the naive man. For the latter, God is a being from whose care one hopes to benefit and whose punishment one fears; a sublimation of a feeling similar to that of a child for its father.

From "The Religious Spirit of Science"; published in *Mein Weltbild*, 1934; reprinted in *Ideas and Opinions*, p. 40

The scientist is possessed by the sense of universal causation. . . . His religious feeling takes the form of a rapturous amazement at the harmony of natural law, which reveals an intelligence of such superiority that, compared with it, all the systematic thinking and acting of human beings is an utterly insignificant reflection. . . . It is beyond question closely akin to that which has possessed the religious geniuses of all ages.

Ibid.

What is the meaning of human life, or for that matter, of the life of any creature? To know an answer to this question means to be religious. You ask: Does it make any sense, then, to pose this question? I answer: The man who regards his own life and that of his fellow creatures as meaningless is not merely unhappy but hardly fit for life.

Published in *Mein Weltbild*, 1934; reprinted in *Ideas and Opinions*, p. 11

Everyone who is seriously involved in the pursuit of science becomes convinced that a spirit is manifest in the laws of the Universe—a spirit vastly superior to that of man. . . . In this way the pursuit of science leads to a religious feeling of a special sort, which is indeed quite different from the religiosity of someone more naive.

Letter to a child who asked if scientists pray, January 24, 1936; Einstein Archive 42-601

Whatever there is of God and goodness in the universe, it must work itself out and express itself through us. We cannot stand aside and let God do it.

From a conversation recorded by Algernon Black, Fall 1940; Einstein Archive 54-834

A religious person is devout in the sense that he has no doubt about the significance of those superpersonal objects and goals which neither require nor are capable of rational foundation.

Nature 146 (1940), p. 605

To [the sphere of religion] belongs the faith in the possibility that the regulations valid for the world of existence are rational, that is, comprehensible to reason. I cannot conceive of a genuine scientist without that profound faith.

From "Science and Religion," a written contribution to a symposium held in New York in 1941 on what contributions science, philosophy, and religion make to the cause of American democracy; Einstein Archive 28-523; in *Ideas and Opinions*, pp. 41–49

Science without religion is lame, religion without science is blind.

Ibid., p. 46 (This may be a play on Kant's "Notion without intuition is empty, intuition without notion is blind")

The main source of the present-day conflicts between the spheres of religion and of science lies in the concept of a personal God.

Ibid., p. 47

In their struggle for the ethical good, teachers of religion must have the stature to give up the doctrine of a personal God, that is, give up that source of fear and hope which in the past placed such vast power in the hands of priests.

Ibid., p. 48

The further the spiritual evolution of mankind advances, the more certain it seems to me that the path to genuine religiosity does not lie through the fear of life, and the fear of death, and blind faith, but through striving after rational knowledge.

Ibid., p. 49

It is quite possible that we can do greater things than Jesus, for what is written in the Bible about him is poetically embellished.

Quoted in W. Hermanns, "A Talk with Einstein," October 1943; Einstein Archive 55-285

No idea is conceived in our mind independent of our five senses [i.e., no idea is divinely inspired].

Ibid.

I would not think that philosophy and reason themselves will be man's guide in the foreseeable future; however, they will remain the most beautiful sanctuary they have always been for the select few.

Letter to Benedetto Croce, June 7, 1944; Einstein Archive 34-075; also quoted in Pais, *Einstein Lived Here*, p. 122

I often read the Bible, but its original text has remained inaccessible to me.

> Letter to H. Friedmann, September 2, 1945, regarding his lack of knowledge of the Hebrew language; quoted in Pais, *Subtle Is the Lord*, p. 38

It is this . . . symbolic content of the religious traditions which is likely to come into conflict with science. . . . Thus it is of vital importance for the preservation of true religion that such conflicts be avoided when they arise from subjects which, in fact, are not really essential for the pursuance of the religious aims.

> Statement to the Liberal Ministers' Club, New York City; published in *The Christian Register*, June 1948

My position concerning God is that of an agnostic. I am convinced that a vivid consciousness of the primary importance of moral principles for the betterment and ennoblement of life does not need the idea of a law-giver, especially a law-giver who works on the basis of reward and punishment.

> Letter to M. Berkowitz, October 25, 1950; Einstein Archive 59-215

I have found no better expression than "religious" for confidence in the rational nature of reality, insofar as it is accessible to human reason. Whenever this feeling is absent, science degenerates into uninspired empiricism.

> Letter to Maurice Solovine, January 1, 1951; Einstein Archive 21-474, 80-871; published in *Letters to Solovine*, p. 119

Mere unbelief in a personal God is no philosophy at all.

> Letter to V. T. Aaltonen, May 7, 1952, on his opinion that belief in a personal God is better than atheism; Einstein Archive 59-059

My feeling is religious insofar as I am imbued with the consciousness of the insufficiency of the human mind to understand more deeply the harmony of the Universe which we try to formulate as "laws of nature."

> Letter to Beatrice Frohlich, December 17, 1952; Einstein Archive 59-797

The idea of a personal God is quite alien to me and seems even naive.

> Ibid.

To assume the existence of an unperceivable being . . . does not facilitate understanding the orderliness we find in the perceivable world.

Letter to an Iowa student who asked, What is God? July 1953; Einstein Archive 59-085

I do not believe in the immortality of the individual, and I consider ethics to be an exclusively human concern with no superhuman authority behind it.

July 1953; Einstein Archive 36-553; also quoted in Dukas and Hoffmann, *Albert Einstein, the Human Side*, p. 39

If God has created the world, his primary worry was certainly not to make its understanding easy for us.

Letter to David Bohm, February 10, 1954; Einstein Archive 8-041

I consider the Society of Friends the religious community which has the highest moral standards. As far as I know, they have never made evil compromises and are always guided by their conscience. In international life, especially, their influence seems to me very beneficial and effective.

Letter to A. Chapple, Australia, February 23, 1954; Einstein Archive 59-405; also quoted in Nathan and Norden, *Einstein on Peace*, p. 510

I do not believe in a personal God and I have never denied this but have expressed it clearly. If something is in me which can be called religious, then it is the unbounded admiration for the structure of the world so far as science can reveal it.

Letter to an admirer, March 22, 1954; Einstein Archive 39-525; also quoted in Dukas and Hoffmann, *Albert Einstein, the Human Side*, p. 43

I am a deeply religious nonbeliever. . . . This is a somewhat new kind of religion.

Letter to Hans Muehsam, March 30, 1954; Einstein Archive 38-434

I don't try to imagine a God; it suffices to stand in awe of the structure of the world, insofar as it allows our inadequate senses to appreciate it.

Letter to S. Flesch, April 16, 1954; Einstein Archive 30-1154

I have never imputed to Nature a purpose or a goal, or anything that could be understood as anthropomorphic. What I see in Nature is a magnificent structure that we can comprehend only very imperfectly, and that must fill a thinking person with a feeling of humility. This is a genuinely religious feeling that has nothing to do with mysticism.

1954 or 1955; quoted in Dukas and Hoffmann, *Albert Einstein, the Human Side*, p. 39

A man's moral worth is not measured by what his religious beliefs are but rather by what emotional impulses he has received from Nature during his lifetime.

To Sister Margrit Goehner, February 1955; Einstein Archive 59-831

Epistemology without contact with science becomes an empty scheme. Science without epistemology is—insofar as it is thinkable at all—primitive and muddled.

Quoted in Schilpp, *Albert Einstein: Philosopher-Scientist*, p. 5

Thus I came . . . to a deep religiosity, which, however, reached an abrupt end at the age of 12. Through the reading of popular scientific books I soon reached a conviction that much in the stories of the Bible could not be true. . . . Suspicion against every kind of authority grew out of this experience . . . an attitude which has never left me.

Ibid., p. 9

Out yonder there was this huge world, which exists independently of us human beings and which stands before us like a great, eternal riddle, at least partially accessible to our inspection and thinking. The contemplation of this world beckoned like a liberation, and I soon noticed that many a man I had learned to esteem and admire had found inner freedom and security in devoted occupation with it.

Ibid., p. 95

Isn't all of philosophy as if written in honey? Something may appear clear at first, but when one looks again it has disappeared. Only the pap remains.

Quoted in Rosenthal-Schneider, *Reality and Scientific Truth*, p. 90

My views are near those of Spinoza: admiration for the beauty and belief in the logical simplicity of the order and harmony which we can grasp humbly and only imperfectly. I believe that we have to content ourselves with our imperfect knowledge and understanding and treat values and moral obligations as purely human problems.

Quoted in Hoffmann, *Albert Einstein: Creator and Rebel*, p. 95

My religion consists of a humble admiration of the illimitable superior spirit who reveals himself in the slight details we are able to perceive with our frail and feeble minds. That deeply emotional conviction of the presence of a superior reasoning power, which is revealed in the incomprehensible universe, forms my idea of God.

Quoted in the *New York Times* obituary, April 19, 1955

On Science and Scientists, Mathematics, and Technology

With H. A. Lorentz and Sir Arthur Eddington, probably in Leyden, 1923. (AIP Emilio Segré Visual Archives)

$E = mc^2$.

Statement of the equivalency of mass and energy—energy equals mass times the speed of light squared—which opened up the atomic age. The original statement was: "If a body releases the energy L in the form of radiation, its mass is decreased by L/V^2." (See *CPAE*, translation volume, Vol. 2, Doc. 24, p. 174, "Does the Inertia of a Body Depend on Its Energy Content?") The equation derives from the special theory of relativity, which played a decisive role in the investigation and development of nuclear energy. A mass can be converted into a vast amount of energy (i.e., when a particle is released from an atom it is converted to energy), demonstrating a fundamental relationship in nature. The theory also introduced a new definition of space and time. Originally in "Ist die Tragheit eines Körpers von seinem Energieinhalt abhängig?" *Annalen der Physik* 18 (1905), pp. 639–641; see *CPAE*, Vol. 2, Doc. 24

From this we conclude that a balance-wheel clock located at the Earth's equator must go more slowly, by a very small amount, than a precisely similar clock situated at one of the poles under otherwise identical conditions.

From "On the Electrodynamics of Moving Bodies"; see *CPAE*, Vol. 2, Doc. 23; trans. on p. 153 of translation volume; originally in "Zur Elektrodynamik bewegter Körper," *Annalen der Physik* 17 (1905), pp. 891–921

Each ray of light moves in the coordinate system "at rest" with the definite, constant velocity *V* independent of whether this ray of light is emitted by a body at rest or a body in motion.

1905; ibid.; see *CPAE*, translation volume, p. 143

Thanks to my having hit upon the fortunate idea of introducing the relativity principle into physics, you (and others) enormously overestimate my scientific abilities, to the point where this makes me somewhat uncomfortable.

Letter to Arnold Sommerfeld, January 14, 1908; *CPAE*, Vol. 5, Doc. 73

People who have been privileged to contribute something to the advancement of science should not let [arguments about priority] becloud their joy over the fruits of common endeavor.

Letter to Johannes Stark, February 22, 1908; *CPAE*, Vol. 5, Doc. 88

The more success the quantum theory has, the sillier it looks.

Letter to Heinrich Zangger, May 20, 1912; *CPAE*, Vol. 5, Doc. 398

I cannot find the time to write because I am occupied with truly great things. Day and night I rack my brain in an effort to penetrate more deeply into the things that I gradually discovered in the past two years and that represent an unprecedented advance in the fundamental problems of physics.

> Letter to Elsa Löwenthal, February 1914, about his work on an extension of his theory of gravitation, the first stage of which was published half a year earlier; *CPAE*, Vol. 5, Doc. 509

The state of mind which enables a man to do work of this kind . . . is akin to that of the religious worshiper or the lover; the daily effort comes from no deliberate intention or program, but straight from the heart.

> From "Principles of Research," speech at Max Planck's sixtieth birthday, 1918; published in *Mein Weltbild*; reprinted in *Ideas and Opinions*, pp. 224–227

I believe with Schopenhauer that one of the strongest motives that leads men to art and science is escape from everyday life with its painful crudity and hopeless dreariness from the fetters of one's own everyday desires. . . . A finely tempered nature longs to escape from personal life into the world of objective perception and thought.

> Ibid.

Then I would feel sorry for the good Lord. The theory is correct anyway.

> In answer to a student's question in 1919 about how he would have reacted if his theory of general relativity had not been confirmed experimentally; quoted in Rosenthal-Schneider, *Reality and Scientific Truth*, p. 74

It is my inner conviction that the development of science seeks in the main to satisfy the longing for pure knowledge.

> 1920; quoted in Moszkowski, *Conversations with Einstein*, p. 173

The word "discovery" in itself is to be deprecated. For discovery is equivalent to becoming aware of a thing which is already formed; this links up with proof, which no longer bears the character of "discovery" but, in the last instance, of the means that leads to discovery. . . . Discovery is really not a creative act.

> Ibid., p. 95

The aspect of knowledge that has not yet been laid bare gives the investigator a feeling akin to that experienced by a child who seeks to grasp the masterly way in which elders manipulate things.

> Ibid., p. 46

Insofar as geometry is certain, it says nothing about the actual world, and insofar as it says something about our experience, it is uncertain.

From a lecture delivered at the Prussian Academy of Sciences, January 27, 1921; quoted in Frank, *Einstein: His Life and Times*, p. 177

The Lord God is subtle, but malicious he is not.

Originally said to Princeton University mathematics professor Oscar Veblen, May 1921, while Einstein was in Princeton for a series of lectures, upon hearing that an experimental result, if true, would contradict his theory of gravitation; the result turned out to be false. Some say by this remark Einstein meant that Nature hides her secrets by being subtle, while others say he meant that Nature is mischievous but not bent on trickery. Permanently inscribed in stone above the fireplace in the faculty lounge, 202 Jones Hall (called Fine Hall until Princeton's new mathematics building by that name was constructed), in the original German: "Raffiniert ist der Herr Gott, aber boshaft ist Er nicht." Quoted widely in various translated versions, e.g., in Pais, *Subtle Is the Lord*; Frank, *Einstein: His Life and Times*, p. 285; and Hoffmann, *Albert Einstein: Creator and Rebel*, p. 146

I have second thoughts. Maybe God *is* malicious.

To Valentine Bargmann, meaning that God makes us believe we have understood something that in reality we are far from understanding; quoted in Sayen, *Einstein in America*, p. 51

Nature conceals her secrets because she is sublime, not because she is a trickster.

> Aphorism scribbled in German in Einstein's hand; newly found in the duplicate Einstein archive in Boston by Joszef Illy

Relativity is purely a scientific matter and has nothing to do with religion.

> In response to the Archbishop of Canterbury's question about "what effect relativity would have on religion," London, 1921; quoted in Frank, *Einstein: His Life and Times*, p. 190

Now to the name "relativity theory." I admit that it is unfortunate, and has given occasion to philosophical misunderstandings.

> Letter to E. Zschimmer, September 30, 1921, referring to the term for his theory, provided by Max Planck, which stuck despite his unhappiness with it. He would have preferred "theory of invariance," which he felt would better describe the *method*, if not the content. See Holton, *The Advancement of Science*, pp. 69, 110, 312n.21

I was sitting in the patent office in Bern when all of a sudden a thought occurred to me: if a person falls freely, he won't feel his own weight. I was startled.

This simple thought made a deep impression on me. It impelled me toward a theory of gravitation.

> In Kyoto lecture, 1922; quoted in J. Ishiwara, *Einstein Koen-Roku* (Tokyo, 1977)

After a certain high level of technical skill is achieved, science and art tend to coalesce in esthetics, plasticity, and form. The greatest scientists are always artists as well.

> Remark made in 1923; recalled by Archibald Henderson, *Durham Morning Herald*, August 21, 1955; Einstein Archive 33-257

The more one chases after quanta, the better they hide themselves.

> Letter to Paul Ehrenfest, July 12, 1924, expressing his frustration over quantum theory; Einstein Archive 10-089

My interest in science was always essentially limited to the study of principles. . . . That I have published so little is due to this same circumstance, as the great need to grasp principles has caused me to spend most of my time on fruitless pursuits.

> Letter to Maurice Solovine, October 30, 1924; Einstein Archive 21-195; published in *Letters to Solovine*, p. 63

Quantum mechanics is very worthy of regard. But an inner voice tells me that this is not the true Jacob. The theory yields much, but it hardly brings us close to the secrets of the Ancient One. In any case, I am convinced that He does not play dice.

> Letter to Max Born, December 4, 1926; Einstein Archive 8-180; also quoted in French, *Einstein: A Centenary Volume*, p. 275

I admire to the highest degree the achievement of the younger generation of physicists which goes by the name of quantum mechanics and believe in the deep level of truth of that theory; but I believe that the restriction to statistical laws will be a passing one.

> From a speech on June 28, 1929, on acceptance of the Planck Medal; quoted in *Forschungen und Fortschritte* 5 (1929), pp. 248–249

Concern for man himself and his fate must always be the chief interest of all technical endeavors . . . in order that the creations of our mind shall be a blessing and not a curse to mankind. Never forget this in the midst of your diagrams and equations.

> From an address at the California Institute of Technology, Pasadena, February 1931; quoted in *New York Times*, February 17, 1931, p. 6:3

Why does this magnificent applied science which saves work and makes life easier bring us so little happiness? The simple answer: because we have not yet learned to make sensible use of it.

Ibid.

The scientist finds his reward in what Henri Poincaré calls the joy of comprehension, and not in the possibilities of application to which any discovery may lead.

From the "Epilogue" to Planck, *Where Is Science Going?* 1932, p. 211

I believe that the present fashion of applying the actions of physical science to human life is not only a mistake but has something reprehensible about it.

On a "worldview" of relativity and the gross abuse of science in areas to which it is not applicable, 1932; ibid.; also quoted by Loren R. Graham in Holton and Elkana, *Albert Einstein: Historical and Cultural Perspectives*, p. 107

The years of searching in the dark for a truth that one feels but cannot express, the intense desire and the alternations of confidence and misgiving until one breaks through to clarity and understanding, are known only to him who has experienced them himself.

From a lecture at the University of Glasgow, June 20, 1933; quoted in *The Origins of the Theory of Relativity*

To be sure, it is not the fruits of scientific research that elevate a man and enrich his nature, but the urge to understand, the intellectual work, creative or receptive.

Published in *Mein Weltbild*, 1934; reprinted in *Ideas and Opinions*, p. 12

The general public may be able to follow the details of scientific research to only a modest degree; but it can register at least one great and important gain: confidence that human thought is dependable and natural law is universal.

From "Science and Society," 1935; quoted in *Einstein on Humanism*, p. 13

The whole of science is nothing more than the refinement of everyday thinking.

From "Physics and Reality," *Franklin Institute Journal* 221, no. 3 (March 1936), pp. 349–382

I still struggle with the same problems as ten years ago. I succeed in small matters but the real goal remains unattainable, even though it sometimes seems palpably close. It is hard yet rewarding: hard because the goal is beyond my powers, but rewarding because it makes one immune to the distractions of everyday life.

Letter to Otto Juliusburger, September 28, 1937; Einstein Archive 38-163

Physical concepts are free creations of the human mind and are not, however it may seem, uniquely determined by the external world.

From *The Evolution of Physics*, with L. Infeld, 1938

What we call physics comprises that group of natural sciences which base their concepts on measurements, and whose concepts and propositions lend themselves to mathematical formulations.

From "The Fundamentals of Theoretical Physics," *Science* 91 (May 24, 1940), pp. 487–492

There has always been present the attempt to find a unifying theoretical basis for all these [various branches of physics] . . . from which all the concepts and relationships of the single disciplines might be derived by logical process. This is what we mean by the search for a foundation of the whole of physics.

The confident belief that this ultimate goal may be reached is the chief source of the passionate devotion which has always animated the researcher.

Ibid.

You cannot love a car the way you love a horse. The horse brings out human feelings the way machines cannot do. Things like machines may develop or neglect certain things in people. . . . Machines make our life impersonal and stultify certain elements in us [and create an] impersonal environment.

From a conversation recorded by Algernon Black, Fall 1940; Einstein Archive 54-834

It is hard to sneak a look at God's cards. But that he would choose to play dice with the world . . . is something that I cannot believe for a single moment.

Letter to Cornelius Lanczos, March 21, 1942, expressing his reaction to quantum theory, which refutes relativity theory by stating that an observer *can* influence reality, that events *do* happen randomly; Einstein Archive 15-294; quoted in Hoffmann, *Albert Einstein: Creator and Rebel*, chap. 10; Frank, *Einstein: His Life and Times*, pp. 208, 285; Pais, *Einstein Lived Here*, p. 114. (Physicist Niels Bohr is said to have told Einstein, "Stop telling God what to do!")

Do not worry about your difficulties in mathematics; I can assure you that mine are still greater.

To junior high school student Barbara Wilson, January 7, 1943; Einstein Archive 42-606; also quoted in Dukas and Hoffmann, *Albert Einstein, the Human Side*, p. 8

The entire history of physics since Galileo bears witness to the importance of the function of the theoretical physicist, from whom the basic theoretical ideas originate. A priori construction in physics is as essential as empirical facts.

Memo, with Hermann Weyl, to the faculty of the Institute for Advanced Study, early 1945, recommending theoretician Wolfgang Pauli over Robert Oppenheimer for a professorship at the Institute; Pauli declined, and Oppenheimer, offered the directorship in 1946, accepted; quoted in Regis, *Who Got Einstein's Office?* p. 135

A scientific person will never understand why he should believe in opinions for the single reason that they are contained in a certain book. . . . He will never believe that the results of his own attempts are final.

Letter to J. Lee, September 10, 1945; Einstein Archive 57-061

I believe that the horrifying deterioration in the ethical conduct of people today stems from the mechanization and dehumanization of our lives—the distastrous by-product of the scientific and technical mentality. Nostra culpa! Man grows cold faster than the planet he inhabits.

Letter to Otto Juliusburger, April 11, 1946; Einstein Archive 38-228

In my scientific work, I am still hampered by the same mathematical difficulties that have been making it impossible for me to confirm or refute my general relativistic field theory. . . . I won't ever solve it; it will be forgotten and must later be discovered again.

Letter to Maurice Solovine, November 25, 1948; Einstein Archive 21-256, 80-865; published in *Letters to Solovine*, pp. 105, 107

The grand aim of all science is to cover the greatest number of empirical facts by logical deduction from the smallest number of hypotheses or axioms.

Quoted in *Life* magazine, January 9, 1950

The unified field theory has been put into retirement. It is so difficult to employ mathematically that I have not been able to verify it somehow, in spite of all my efforts. This state of affairs will no doubt last many more years, mostly because physicists have little understanding for logical-philosophical arguments.

> Letter to Maurice Solovine, February 12, 1951; Einstein Archive 21-277; published in *Letters to Solovine*, p. 123

Science is a wonderful thing if one does not have to earn a living at it. One should earn one's living by work of which one is sure one is capable. Only when we do not have to be accountable to anyone can we find joy in scientific endeavor.

> Letter to a California student, 1951; quoted in Dukas and Hoffmann, *Albert Einstein, the Human Side*, p. 57

Betterment of conditions the world over is not essentially dependent on scientific knowledge but on the fulfillment of human traditions and ideals.

> 1952; quoted in French, *Einstein: A Centenary Volume*, p. 197

Development of Western science is based on two great achievements: the invention of the formal logical system (in Euclidean geometry) by the Greek philosophers, and the discovery of the possibility to find out causal relationships by systematic experiment (during the Renaissance).

Letter to J. S. Switzer, April 23, 1953; Einstein Archive 61-381

That no one can make a definite statement about its [unified field theory's] confirmation or nonconfirmation results from the fact that there are no methods of affirming anything with respect to solutions that do not yield to the peculiarities of such a complicated nonlinear system of equations. It is even possible that no one will ever know.

Letter to Maurice Solovine, May 28, 1953; Einstein Archive 21-300; published in *Letters to Solovine*, p. 149

In striving to do scientific work the chance—even for very gifted persons—to achieve something of real value is very little. . . . There is only one way out: give most of your time to some practical work . . . that agrees with your nature, and spend the rest of it in study. So you will be able . . . to lead a normal and harmonious life even without the special blessings of the Muses.

Letter to a man from India who was unsure about what lifework to pursue, July 14, 1953; quoted in Dukas and Hoffmann, *Albert Einstein, the Human Side*, p. 59

Strange that science, which in the old days seemed harmless, should have evolved into a nightmare that causes everyone to tremble.

Letter to Queen Elizabeth of Belgium, March 28, 1954; Einstein Archive 32-410; quoted in Whitrow, *Einstein*, p. 89

I believe that every true theorist is a kind of tamed metaphysicist, no matter how pure a "positivist" he may fancy himself.

From "On the Generalized Theory of Gravitation," *Scientific American* 182, no. 4 (April 1954)

Science will stagnate if it is made to serve practical goals.

Quoted in Nathan and Norden, *Einstein on Peace*, p. 402

Men really devoted to the progress of knowledge concerning the physical world . . . never worked for practical, let alone military, goals.

Ibid., p. 510

It appears dubious that a [classical] field theory can account for the atomistic structure of matter and radiation as well as of quantum phenomena. Most physicists will reply with a convinced "No," since they believe that the quantum problem has been solved in principle by other means. However that may be, Lessing's comforting words stay with us: The aspiration to truth is more precious than its assured possession.

Einstein's final written scientific words, on quantum theory; quoted in Seelig, *Helle Zeit, Dunkle Zeit*

The normal adult never bothers his head about spacetime problems. Everything that there is to be thought about, in his opinion, has already been done in early childhood. I, on the contrary, developed so slowly that I only began to wonder about space and time when I was already grown up. In consequence, I probed deeper into the problem than an ordinary child would have done.

Ibid., p. 71

I have thought a hundred times as much about the quantum problems as I have about general relativity theory.

To Otto Stern, quoted by Res Jost in Pais, "Einstein, Newton, and Success," in French, *Einstein: A Centenary Volume*, p. 37

I can, if the worse comes to the worst, still realize that God may have created a world in which there are no natural laws. In short, a chaos. But that there should be statistical laws with definite solutions, i.e., laws that compel God to throw dice in each individual case, I find highly disagreeable.

To James Franck, quoted by C. P. Snow in French, *Einstein: A Centenary Volume*, p. 6

One thing I have learned in a long life: that all our science, measured against reality, is primitive and childlike—and yet it is the most precious thing we have.

Quoted in Hoffmann, *Albert Einstein: Creator and Rebel*, p. v

It follows from the theory of relativity that mass and energy are both different manifestations of the same thing—a somewhat unfamiliar conception for the average man. Furthermore, $E = mc^2$, in which energy is put equal to mass multiplied with the square of the velocity of light, showed that a very small amount of mass may be converted into a very large amount of energy . . . the mass and energy in fact were equivalent.

Read aloud to an audience, filmed and shown in the Einstein film produced by Nova Television, 1979

Physics is essentially an intuitive and concrete science. Mathematics is only a means for expressing the laws that govern phenomena.

Quoted by M. Solovine in "Introduction" to *Letters to Solovine*, pp. 7–8

In the beginning (if there was such a thing), God created Newton's laws of motion together with the necessary masses and forces. This is all; everything beyond this follows from the development of appropriate mathematical methods by means of deduction.

Quoted in Schilpp, *Autobiographical Notes*, p. 19

A theory is the more impressive the greater the simplicity of its premises, the more different kinds of things it relates, and the more extended its area of applicability.

Ibid., p. 33

An hour sitting with a pretty girl on a park bench passes like a minute, but a minute sitting on a hot stove seems like an hour.

Einstein's explanation of relativity given to his secretary, Helen Dukas, to relay to reporters and other laypersons; quoted in Sayen, *Einstein in America*, p. 130

The aim of science is, on the one hand, as complete a comprehension as possible of the connection between perceptible experiences in their totality, and, on the other hand, the achievement of this aim by employing a minimum of primary concepts and relations.

Quoted in Cuny, *Albert Einstein*, p. 129

I have little patience for scientists who take a board of wood, look for its thinnest part, and drill a great number of holes when the drilling is easy.

Related by Philipp Frank in "Einstein's Philosophy of Science," *Reviews of Modern Physics* (1949)

A scientist is a mimosa when he himself has made a mistake, and a roaring lion when he discovers a mistake of others.

Quoted in Ehlers, *Liebes Hertz!* p. 45

On Miscellaneous Subjects

Einstein in the parlor of his Princeton home, dressed for a New York appointment, early 1938. (Lotte Jacobi Archives, University of New Hampshire)

ABORTION

A woman should be able to choose to have an abortion up to a certain point in pregnancy.

To the World League for Sexual Reform, Berlin, September 6, 1929; Einstein Archive 48-304; also quoted in Grüning, *Ein Haus für Albert Einstein*, p. 305

ACHIEVEMENT

The value of achievement lies in the achieving.

October 1950; Einstein Archive 60-297

AGING

There is, after all, something eternal that lies beyond the reach of the hand of fate and of all human delusions. And such eternals lie closer to an older person than to a younger one who oscillates between fear and hope.

Letter to Queen Elizabeth of Belgium, March 20, 1936; Einstein Archive 32-387; quoted in *Einstein: A Portrait*, p. 54

People like you and I, though mortal of course, like everyone else, do not grow old no matter how long we live. What I mean is that we never cease to stand like curious children before the great Mystery into which we were born.

Letter to Otto Juliusburger, September 29, 1942; Einstein Archive 38-238

I am content in my later years. I have kept my good humor and take neither myself nor the next person seriously.

Letter to P. Moos, March 30, 1950; Einstein Archive 60-587

I have always loved solitude, a trait which tends to increase with age.

Letter to E. Marangoni, October 1, 1952; Einstein Archive 60-406

If younger people were not taking care of me, I would surely try to be institutionalized, so that I would not have to become so concerned about the decline of my physical and mental powers, which after all is unpreventable in the natural course of things.

Letter to W. Lebach, May 12, 1953; Einstein Archive 60-221

In one's youth every person and every event appear to be unique. With age one becomes much more aware that similar events recur. Later on one is less often delighted or surprised, but also less disappointed than in earlier years.

Letter to Queen Elizabeth of Belgium, January 3, 1954; Einstein Archive 32-408

I believe that older people who have scarcely anything to lose ought to be willing to speak out on behalf of those who are young and who are subject to much greater restraint.

Letter to Queen Elizabeth of Belgium, March 28, 1954; Einstein Archive 32-411

Every age has its beautiful moments.

To Margot Einstein, quoted in Sayen, *Einstein in America*, p. 298

I live in that solitude which is painful in youth, but delicious in the years of maturity.

Quoted in *Out of My Later Years*, p. 13

AMBITION

Nothing truly valuable arises from ambition or from a mere sense of duty; it stems rather from love and devotion towards men and towards objective things.

Statement for an Idaho farmer requesting some words that his son, Albert Wada, could live by as he grew up, July 30, 1947; Einstein Archive 58-934; quoted in Dukas and Hoffmann, *Albert Einstein, the Human Side*, p. 46

ANIMALS / PETS

Thank you very much for your kind and interesting information. I am sending my heartiest greetings to my namesake, also from our tomcat, who was very interested in the story and even a little jealous. The reason is that his own name, "Tiger," does not express, as in your case, the close kinship to the Einstein family.

Letter to Edward Moses, August 10, 1946, after learning that his ship's crew had rescued a kitten in Germany and named it Einstein; Einstein Archive 57-194

I know what's wrong, dear fellow, but I don't know how to turn it off.

To his tomcat, Tiger, who seemed depressed because he was housebound due to rain; recalled by Ernst Straus in memorial talk, "Albert Einstein: The Man," at UCLA, May 1955, pp. 14–15

The main thing is that *he* knows.

> About a friend's dog, Moses, whose long fur made it difficult to tell one end from the other; January 15, 1979, interview with Margot Einstein by J. Sayen, quoted in Sayen, *Einstein in America*, p. 131

The dog is very smart. He feels sorry for me because I receive so much mail; that's why he tries to bite the mailman.

> Regarding his dog, Chico; quoted in Ehlers, *Liebes Hertz!* p. 162

BIRTH CONTROL

I am convinced that some political and social activities and practices of the Catholic organizations are detrimental and even dangerous for the community as a whole, here and everywhere. I mention here only the fight against birth control at a time when overpopulation in various countries has become a serious threat to the health of people and a grave obstacle to any attempt to organize peace on this planet.

> Letter to a reader of the *Brooklyn Tablet*, 1954, who questioned Einstein about whether he had been correctly quoted on the subject

BIRTHDAYS

My dear little sweetheart . . . first, my belated cordial congratulations on your birthday yesterday, which I forgot once again.

Letter to girlfriend Mileva Marić, December 19, 1901; *CPAE,* Vol. 1, Doc. 130

Such celebrations are for children.

New York Times, March 14, 1950

BLACKS / RACISM

This country still has a heavy debt to discharge for all the troubles and disabilities it has laid on the Negro's shoulder. . . . To the Negro and his wonderful songs and choirs we owe the finest contribution in the realm of art which America has given the world.

At dedication of the Wall of Fame at 1940 World's Fair

[Bias against the Negro] is the worst disease from which the society of our nation suffers.

Quoted in the *New York Times,* September 25, 1946

Security against lynching is one of the most urgent tasks of our generation.

To President Harry Truman, quoted in the *New York Times*, September 23, 1946

BOOKS

What I have to say about this book can be found inside the book.

Reply to a *New York Times* reporter's request for a comment on his book *The Evolution of Physics*, written with Leopold Infeld; quoted by Ehlers, *Liebes Hertz!* p. 65

CLOTHES

If I were to start taking care of my grooming, I would no longer be my own self. . . . So the hell with it. If you find me so repulsive, then look for a friend who is more appealing to female tastes. But I will continue to be unconcerned about it, which surely has the advantage that I'm left in peace by many a fop who would otherwise come to see me.

Letter to future second wife, Elsa Löwenthal, after December 2, 1913; *CPAE*, Vol. 5, Doc. 489

I like neither new clothes nor new kinds of food.

1920, recalled by E. Salaman, *Encounter*, 1979; quoted in Pais, *Subtle Is the Lord*, p. 16

It would be a sad situation if the wrapper were better than the meat wrapped inside it.

Recalled in the *New York Times*, April 19, 1955, about Einstein's notorious disregard for his outward appearance

"Why should I? Everyone knows me there" (upon being told by his wife to dress properly when going to the office). "Why should I? No one knows me there" (upon being told to dress properly for his first big conference).

Quoted in Ehlers, *Liebes Hertz!* p. 87

I have reached an age when, if someone tells me to wear socks, I don't have to.

Quoted by neighbor and fellow physicist Allan Shenstone, in Sayen, *Einstein in America*, p. 69

When I was young, I found out that the big toe always ends up making a hole in a sock. So I stopped wearing socks.

To Philippe Halsman, quoted in French, *Einstein: A Centenary Volume*, p. 27

COMPETITION

I no longer need to take part in the competition of the big brains. Participating [in the process] has always seemed to me to be an awful type of slavery no less evil than the passion for money or power.

Letter to Paul Ehrenfest, May 25, 1927, regarding the rat race for academic promotions; Einstein Archive 10-163; also quoted in Dukas and Hoffmann, *Albert Einstein, the Human Side*, p. 60

COMPREHENSIBILITY

The eternal mystery of the world is its comprehensibility. . . . The fact that it is comprehensible is a miracle.

From "Physics and Reality," *Franklin Institute Journal* 221, no. 3 (March 1936), pp. 349–382; reprinted in *Ideas and Opinions*, p. 292 (popularly paraphrased as, "The most incomprehensible thing about the universe is that it is comprehensible")

CONSCIENCE

Never do anything against conscience even if the state demands it.

Recalled in *Saturday Review* obituary, April 30, 1955

CREATIVITY

The monotony of a quiet life stimulates the creative mind.

From a speech, "Civilization and Science," at Royal Albert Hall, London, October 3, 1933; quoted in *The Times* (London), October 4, 1933, p. 14

Without creative personalities able to think and judge independently, the upward development of society is as unthinkable as the development of the individual personality without the nourishing soil of the community.

Published in *Mein Weltbild*, 1934; reprinted in *Ideas and Opinions*, p. 14

True art is characterized by an irresistible urge in the creative artist.

November 15, 1950, regarding musician Ernst Bloch; Einstein Archive 34-332; also quoted in Dukas and Hoffmann, *Albert Einstein, the Human Side*, p. 77

CRIMINALS

I think we have to safeguard ourselves against people who are a menace to others, quite apart from what may have motivated their deeds.

Letter to Otto Juliusburger, April 11, 1946; Einstein Archive 38-228

CURIOSITY

The important thing is not to stop questioning. Curiosity has its own reason for existing. One cannot help but be in awe when he contemplates the mysteries of eternity, of life, of the marvelous structure of reality. It is enough if one tries merely to comprehend a little of this mystery every day. Never lose a holy curiosity.

Personal memoir of William Miller, an editor, quoted in *Life* magazine, May 2, 1955

Curiosity is a delicate little plant which, aside from stimulation, stands mainly in need of freedom.

Quoted in Cline, *Men Who Made a New Physics*, p. 64

DEATH PENALTY

I have reached the conviction that the abolition of the death penalty is desirable. Reasons: (1) Irreparability in the event of an error of justice; (2) detrimental moral influence on those who . . . have to carry out the procedure.

Letter to a Berlin publisher, November 3, 1927; Einstein Archive 46-009. However, several months earlier, according to the *New York Times*: "Professor Einstein does not favor the abolition of the death penalty. . . . He could not see why society should not rid itself of individuals proved socially harmful. He added that society had no greater right to condemn a person to life imprisonment than it had to sentence him to death" (see the *New York Times*, March 6, 1927; also noted in Pais, *Einstein Lived Here*, p. 174)

I am not for punishment at all, but only for measures that save society and for its protection. In principle, I would not be opposed to killing individuals who are worthless or dangerous in that sense. I am against it only because I do not trust people, i.e., the courts. What I value in life is quality rather than quantity.

Letter to Valentin Bulgakov, November 4, 1931; Einstein Archive 45-702

ENGLISH

I cannot write in English, because of the treacherous spelling. When I am reading, I only hear it and am unable to remember what the written word looks like.

Letter to Max Born, September 7, 1944; Einstein Archive 8-208

FLYING SAUCERS

Those people have seen *something*. What it is I do not know and I am not curious to know.

Letter to L. Gardner, July 23, 1952; Einstein Archive 59-803. (Einstein also thought that people should not read science fiction—that it distorts science and gives people the *illusion* of understanding science; see letter to a boy in Iowa, Einstein Archive, 59th reel)

FORCE

Force always attracts men of low morality, and I believe it to be an invariable rule that tyrants of genius are succeeded by scoundrels.

From "What I Believe," *Forum and Century* 84 (1930), pp. 193–194; reprinted in *Ideas and Opinions*, pp. 8–11

GAMES

I do not play games. . . . There is no time for it. When I get through with work I don't want anything that requires the working of the mind.

New York Times, March 28, 1936

GOOD ACTS

Good acts are like good poems. One may easily get their drift, but they are not always rationally understood.

Letter to Maurice Solovine, April 9, 1947; Einstein Archive 21-250; published in *Letters to Solovine*, pp. 99, 101

HOME

It is not so important where one settles down. . . . I myself have wandered continually hither and yon—a stranger everywhere. . . . The ideal of a man such as I am is to be at home anywhere.

Letter to Max Born, March 3, 1920; Einstein Archive 8-146

HOMOSEXUALITY

Homosexuality should not be punishable except to protect children.

Letter to the World League for Sexual Reform, Berlin, September 6, 1929; Einstein Archive 48-304; also quoted in Grüning, *Ein Haus für Albert Einstein*, pp. 305–306

INDIVIDUALS / INDIVIDUALITY

The really valuable thing in the pageant of human life seems to me not the political state, but the creative, sentient individual, the personality; it alone creates the noble and sublime, while the herd as such remains dull in thought and dull in feeling.

From "What I Believe," *Forum and Century* 84 (1930), pp. 193–194; reprinted in *Ideas and Opinions*, pp. 8–11

Valuable achievement can sprout from human society only when it is sufficiently loosened to make possible the free development of an individual's abilities.

From an unpublished article on tolerance, 1934; Einstein Archive 49-094

While it is true that an inherently free . . . person may be destroyed, such an individual can never be enslaved or used as a blind tool.

Statement in *Impact*, UNESCO, 1950

It is important for the common good to foster individuality: for only the individual can produce the new ideas which the community needs for its continuous improvement and needs—indeed, to avoid sterility and petrification.

From a message for a Ben Schemen Dinner, March 1952; Einstein Archive 28-932

INTELLIGENCE

It is abhorrent to me when a fine intelligence is paired with an unsavory character.

Letter to Jakob Laub, May 19, 1909; *CPAE*, Vol. 5, Doc. 161

INTUITION

All great achievements of science start from intuitive knowledge, namely, in axioms, from which deductions are then made. . . . Intuition is the necessary condition for the discovery of such axioms.

Quoted in Moszkowski, *Conversations with Einstein*, p. 180

LIES

He who has never been deceived by a lie does not know the meaning of bliss.

Letter to Elsa Löwenthal, April 30, 1912; *CPAE*, Vol. 5, Doc. 389

LOVE

Love brings much happiness, much more so than pining for someone brings pain.

Letter to Marie Winteler, his first girlfriend, April 21, 1896 (at age 17); *CPAE*, Vol. 1, Doc. 18

Where there is love, there is no imposition.

To editor and friend, Saxe Commins, Summer 1953; quoted in Sayen, *Einstein in America*, p. 294

I am sorry that you are having difficulties bringing your girlfriend [from Dublin to the United States]. But as long as she is there and you are here, you should be able to maintain a splendid relationship. So why do you want to press the issue?

Letter to Cornel Lanczos, February 14, 1955; Einstein Archive 15-328

MARRIAGE

My parents . . . think of a wife as a man's luxury, which he can afford only when he is making a comfortable living. I have a low opinion of this view of the relationship between man and wife, because it makes the wife and the prostitute distinguishable only insofar as the former is able to secure a lifelong contract from the man because of her favorable social rank.

Letter to Mileva Marić, August 6, 1900; *Love Letters*, p. 23; *CPAE*, Vol. 1, Doc. 70

Why should one not admit a man [to the United States] who dares to oppose every war except the inevitable one with his own wife?

Said jokingly to an Associated Press reporter in 1932, upon being informed that some women's clubs were opposed to his visit to the United States for fear he would help spread subversive doctrines such as pacifism; quoted in Frank, *Einstein: His Life and Times*, p. 126

Marriage is the unsuccessful attempt to make something lasting out of an incident.

Quoted by Otto Nathan, April 10, 1982, in an interview with J. Sayen for *Einstein in America*, p. 80

All marriages are dangerous.

Ibid., p. 70

Marriage is but slavery made to appear civilized.

Quoted in Grüning, *Ein Haus für Albert Einstein*, p. 159

Marriage makes people treat each other as articles of property and no longer as free human beings.

Ibid.

MATERIALISM

Human beings can attain a worthy and harmonious life only if they are able to rid themselves, within the limits of human nature, of the striving for the wish fulfillments of material kinds. The goal is to raise the spiritual values of society.

At a planning conference in Princeton of American Friends of Hebrew University; quoted in the *New York Times*, September 20, 1954

MIRACLES

I admit thoughts influence the body.

Einstein Archive 55-285

MORALITY

One must shy away from questionable undertakings, even when they bear a high-sounding name.

Letter to Maurice Solovine, Spring 1923, on Einstein's resignation from a League of Nations commission; Einstein Archive 21-189; published in *Letters to Solovine*, p. 59

Morality is of the highest importance—but for us, not for God.

Letter to a banker in Colorado, August 1927; quoted in Dukas and Hoffmann, *Albert Einstein, the Human Side*, p. 66

The content of scientific theory itself offers no moral foundation for the personal conduct of life.

In *Forum* 83 (1930), p. 373

There is nothing divine about morality; it is a purely human affair.

Published in *Mein Weltbild*, 1934; reprinted in *Ideas and Opinions*, p. 40

Humanity has every reason to place the proclaimers of high moral standards and values above the discoverers of objective truth. What humanity owes to personalities like Buddha, Moses, and Jesus ranks for me higher than all the achievements of the inquiring constructive mind.

Statement in September 1937; quoted in Dukas and Hoffmann, *Albert Einstein, the Human Side*, p. 70

Morality is not a fixed and stark system. . . . It is a task never finished, something always present to guide our judgment and inspire our conduct.

From a commencement address at Swarthmore College, Pennsylvania, June 6, 1938; quoted in the *New York Times*, June 7, 1938

The most important human endeavor is the striving for morality in our actions. Our inner balance and even our very existence depend on it. Only morality in our actions can give beauty and dignity to life.

Letter to a minister in Brooklyn, November 20, 1950; Einstein Archive 28-894, 59-871; quoted in Dukas and Hoffmann, *Albert Einstein, the Human Side*, p. 95

MUSIC

Music does not *influence* research work, but both are nourished by the same sort of longing, and they complement each other in the release they offer.

Letter to Paul Plaut, October 23, 1928; Einstein Archive 28-065; quoted in Dukas and Hoffmann, *Albert Einstein, the Human Side*, p. 78

Mozart wrote such nonsense here!

While struggling to play a piece by Mozart; quoted by Margot Einstein in an interview with J. Sayen for *Einstein in America*, p. 139

First I improvise and if that doesn't help, then I seek solace in Mozart; but when I'm improvising and it appears that something may come of it, I require the clear constructions of Bach in order to follow through.

Explaining how he relaxes after work playing his violin, "Lina," in his Berlin kitchen because of the room's superior acoustics; quoted in Ehlers, *Liebes Hertz!* p. 132

THE MYSTERIOUS

The fairest thing we can experience is the mysterious. It is the fundamental emotion which stands at the cradle of true art and true science. He who does not know it and can no longer wonder, no longer feel amazement, is as good as dead, a snuffed-out candle.

From "What I Believe," *Forum and Century* 84 (1930), pp. 193–194; reprinted in *Ideas and Opinions*, pp. 8–11

PIPE SMOKING

Pipe smoking contributes to a somewhat calm and objective judgment of human affairs.

Upon accepting life membership in the Montreal Pipe Smokers Club; quoted in the *New York Times*, March 12, 1950 (Einstein was said to be so fond of his pipe that he held on to it even after he fell into the water during a boating accident; see Ehlers, *Liebes Hertz!* p. 149)

THE PRESS

The press, which is mostly controlled by vested interests, has an excessive influence on public opinion.

From an interview for the *Nieuwe Rotterdamsche Courant*, 1921; also quoted in *Berliner Tageblatt*, July 7, 1921; reprinted in *Ideas and Opinions*, pp. 3–7

PROHIBITION

Nothing is more destructive of respect for the government and the law of the land than passing laws which cannot be enforced. It is an open secret that the dangerous increase of crime in this country is closely connected with this.

Ibid.

I don't drink, so it's all the same to me.

Statement on Prohibition, perhaps made jokingly, at a press conference on arrival in New York, 1930; shown in A&E Television Einstein Biography, VPI International, 1991; also shown in the Einstein film produced by Nova Television, 1979

PSYCHOANALYSIS

I should like very much to remain in the darkness of not having been analyzed.

1927; quoted in Dukas and Hoffmann, *Albert Einstein, the Human Side*, p. 35

SAILING

The sport which demands the least energy.

Quoted by A. P. French, in French, *Einstein: A Centenary Volume*, p. 61

SCULPTURE

The ability to portray people from motion and in motion requires the highest measure of intuition and talent.

Quoted in Grüning, *Ein Haus für Albert Einstein*, p. 240

SEX EDUCATION

Regarding sex education: no secrets.

Letter to the World League for Sexual Reform, Berlin, September 6, 1929; Einstein Archive 48-304; also quoted in ibid., pp. 305–306

Sailing, a favorite pastime, at Huntington, Long Island, 1937. (Lotte Jacobi Archives, University of New Hampshire)

SLAVERY

Insofar as we may at all claim that slavery has been abolished today, we owe its abolition to the practical consequences of science.

From "Science and Society," 1935; quoted in *Einstein on Humanism*, p. 11

SUCCESS

Try not to become a man of success, but rather try to become a man of value.

Quoted in *Life* magazine, May 2, 1955

THINKING

Words or language, as they are written or spoken, do not seem to play any role in my mechanism of thought.

1945; from Appendix 2 in Hadamard, *An Essay on the Psychology of Invention in the Mathematical Field*

I vill a little t'ink.

Banesh Hoffmann recounting the phrase Einstein used when he needed more time to think about something; quoted in French, *Einstein: A Centenary Volume*, p. 153

I have no doubt that our thinking goes on for the most part without use of signs (words), and beyond that to a considerable degree unconsciously. For how, otherwise, should it happen that sometimes we "wonder" quite spontaneously about some experience? This "wondering" appears to occur when an experience comes into conflict with a world of concepts that is already sufficiently fixed within us.

Quoted in Schilpp, *Autobiographical Notes*, pp. 7–9

TOLERANCE

The most important kind of tolerance is tolerance of the individual by society and the state. . . . When the state becomes the main thing and the individual becomes its weak-willed tool, then all finer values are lost.

From an unpublished article on tolerance, 1934;
Einstein Archive 49-094

TRUTH

The search for truth and knowledge is one of the highest qualities of man—though often the pride in such is most loudly voiced by those who strive for it the least.

From "The Goal of Human Existence," broadcast
for the United Jewish Appeal, April 11, 1943;
Einstein Archive 28-587

It is difficult to say what truth is, but sometimes so easy to recognize a falsehood.

Letter to Jeremiah McGuire, October 24, 1953; Einstein Archive 60-483

Whoever is careless with truth in small matters cannot be trusted in important affairs.

Quoted in Nathan and Norden, *Einstein on Peace,* p. 640

VEGETARIANISM

I have always eaten animal flesh with a somewhat guilty conscience.

August 1953; Einstein Archive 60-058

When you buy a piece of land to plant your cabbage and apples, you first have to drain it; that will kill all water life. Later you would have to kill all the caterpillars etc. that would otherwise eat your plants. If you must avoid all this killing on moral grounds, you will in the end have to kill yourself, all for the sake of leaving alive those creatures who have no notion of moral principles.

Quoted in *Vegetarisches Universum,* December 1957

VIOLENCE

Violence sometimes may have cleared away obstructions quickly, but it never has proved itself creative.

From "Was Europe a Success?" quoted in *Einstein on Humanism*, p. 49

WEALTH

The trite objects of human efforts—possessions, outward success, luxury—have always seemed to me contemptible.

From "What I Believe," in *Forum and Century* 84 (1930), pp. 193–194; reprinted in *Ideas and Opinions*, pp. 8–11

I am absolutely convinced that no wealth in the world can help humanity forward, even in the hands of the most devoted worker in this cause. The example of great and pure personages is the only thing that can lead us to fine ideas and noble deeds. Money only appeals to selfishness and always irresistibly tempts its owner to abuse it. Can anyone imagine Moses, Jesus, or Gandhi with the money-bags of Carnegie?

Published in *Mein Weltbild*, 1934; reprinted in *Ideas and Opinions*, pp. 12–13

The economists will have to revise their theories of value.

Upon being told that two of his handwritten manuscripts fetched $11.5 million at an auction for the war bonds effort; recounted by Julian Boyd to Dorothy Pratt, February 11, 1944, Princeton University Archives; quoted in Sayen, *Einstein in America*, p. 150

All I'll want in my dining room is a pine table, a bench, and a few chairs.

Quoted in Maja Einstein's biography of her brother; also quoted in Dukas and Hoffmann, *Albert Einstein, the Human Side*, p. 14

WISDOM

Wisdom is not a product of schooling but of the lifelong attempt to acquire it.

Letter to an admirer, March 22, 1954; quoted in Dukas and Hoffmann, *Albert Einstein, the Human Side*, p. 44

WOMEN

Very few women are creative. I would not send a daughter of mine to study physics. I'm glad my wife doesn't know any science; my first wife did.

Quoted by Esther Salaman, a young student in Berlin, in the *Listener*, September 8, 1968; also quoted in Highfield and Carter, *The Private Lives*, p. 158

As in all other directions, in science the way should be made easy for women. Yet it must not be taken amiss if I regard the possible results with a certain amount of skepticism. I am referring to certain obstacles in a woman's system which we must regard as given by Nature and which forbid us from applying the same standard of expectation to women as to men.

Quoted in Moszkowski, *Conversations with Einstein*, p. 79

When women are in their homes, they are attached to their furnishings . . . they are always fussing with them. When I am with a woman on a journey, I am the only piece of furniture that she has available, and she cannot refrain from moving around me all day long and improving something about me.

Quoted in Frank, *Einstein: His Life and Times*, p. 126

WORK

Work is the only thing that gives substance to life.

Letter to son Hans Albert, January 4, 1937; Einstein Archive 75-926

It is really a puzzle what drives one to take one's work so devilishly seriously. For whom? For oneself? One soon leaves, after all. For one's companions? For posterity? *No.* It remains a puzzle.

Letter to Joseph Scharl, an artist friend, December 27, 1949; Einstein Archive 34-207

I am also convinced that one gains the purest joy from spiritual things only when they are not tied in with one's livelihood.

Letter to L. Manners, March 19, 1954; Einstein Archive 60-401

YOUTH

O, Youth: Do you know that yours is not the first generation to yearn for a life full of beauty and freedom? Do you know that all your ancestors have felt the same as you do—and fell victim to trouble and hatred? Do you know also that your fervent wishes can only find fulfillment if you succeed in attaining love and understanding of people, and animals, and plants, and stars, so that every joy becomes your joy and every pain your pain?

Written into a neighbor's autograph album in Caputh, Germany, 1932

Attributed to Einstein

Actor Walter Matthau as Einstein in the movie *I.Q.*
(Courtesy of Paramount Pictures. *I.Q.* © 1994
Paramount Pictures. All rights reserved)

An empty stomach is not a good political adviser.

I have survived two wars, two wives, and Hitler.

I do not know how the Third World War will be fought, but I do know how the Fourth will: with sticks and stones.

In any conflict between humanity and technology, humanity will win.

Few people are capable of expressing with equanimity opinions which differ from the prejudices of their social environment.

Imagination is more important than knowledge. Knowledge is limited; imagination encircles the world.

Nothing will benefit human health and increase the chances for survival of life on Earth as much as the evolution of a vegetarian diet.

The discovery of a nuclear chain reaction need not bring about the destruction of mankind any more than the discovery of matches.

It is easier to denature plutonium than to denature the evil spirit of man.

The process of scientific discovery is, in effect, a continual flight from wonder.

Everything that is really great and inspiring is created by the individual who can labor in freedom.

Perfection of means and confusion of ends seem to characterize our age.

It would be possible to describe everything scientifically, but it would make no sense. It would be a description without meaning—as if you described a Beethoven symphony as a variation of wave pressure.

No amount of experimentation can ever prove me right; a single experiment can prove me wrong.

In science the work of the individual is so bound up with that of his scientific predecessors and contemporaries that it appears almost as an impersonal product of his generation.

The effort to get at the truth has to precede all other efforts.

When the blind beetle crawls over the surface of a globe, it doesn't notice that the track it has covered is curved. I was lucky enough to have spotted it.

International law exists only in textbooks on international law.

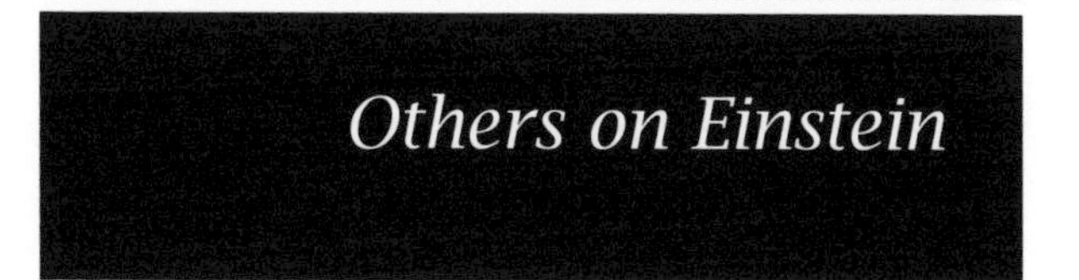

Others on Einstein

In the Grand Canyon, Arizona, February 28, 1931, at Hopi House, with Elsa and Hopi Indians, who called him the "Great Relative." Was the pun intentional? (New York Times Pictures)

Tell me what to do if he says yes. I had to offer the post to him because it's impossible not to. But if he accepts, we are in for trouble.

Ben Gurion to Yitzak Navon, after Abba Eban was instructed to offer the presidency of Israel to Einstein in November 1952; quoted in Holton and Elkana, *Albert Einstein: Historical and Cultural Perspectives*, p. 295

When something struck him as funny, his eyes twinkled merrily and he laughed with his whole being. . . . He was ready for humor.

Algernon Black, 1940; Einstein Archive 54-834

Through Albert Einstein's work the horizon of mankind has been immeasurably widened, at the same time as our world picture has attained a unity and harmony never dreamed of before. The background for such achievement was created by preceding generations of the world community of scientists, and its full consequences will only be revealed to coming generations.

Niels Bohr, *New York Times*, April 19, 1955

Einstein would be one of the greatest theoretical physicists of all time even if he had not written a single line on relativity.

> Max Born, quoted in Hoffmann, *Albert Einstein: Creator and Rebel*, p. 7

He always took his celebrity with humor and laughed at himself.

> Family friend Thomas Bucky, shown in A&E Television Einstein Biography, VPI International, 1991

The contrast between his soft speech and ringing laughter was enormous. . . . Every time he made a point he liked, or heard something that appealed to him, he would burst into a booming laughter that would echo from wall to wall. . . . I had been prepared . . . to know what he would look like . . . but I was totally unprepared for this roaring, booming, friendly, all-enveloping laughter.

> I. Bernard Cohen, quoted in an interview with Whitrow, in Whitrow, *Einstein*, p. 83

I was able to appreciate the clarity of his mind, the breadth of his documentation, and the profundity of his knowledge. . . . One has every right to build the greatest hopes on him and to see in him one of the leading theoreticians of the future.

> Marie Curie, 1911, quoted in Hoffmann, *Albert Einstein: Creator and Rebel*, pp. 98–99

Einstein was prone to talk about God so often that I was led to suspect he was a closet theologian.

Friedrich Dürrenmatt in *Albert Einstein: Ein Vortrag,* p. 12

The professor never wears socks. Even when he was invited by Mr. Roosevelt to the White House he didn't wear socks.

Helen Dukas, recalled by Philippe Halsman in French, *Einstein: A Centenary Volume,* p. 27

It is not ideal to be the wife of a genius. Your life does not belong to you. It seems to belong to everyone else. Nearly every minute of the day I give to my husband, and that means to the public.

Elsa Einstein, as quoted in the *New York Times,* December 22, 1936, two days after her death

Probably the only project he ever gave up on was me. He tried to give me advice, but he soon discovered that I was too stubborn and that he was just wasting his time.

Hans Albert Einstein, *New York Times,* July 27, 1973; quoted in Pais, *Einstein Lived Here,* p. 199

He was very fond of nature. He did not care for large, impressive mountains, but he liked surroundings that were gentle and colorful and gave one lightness of spirit.

Hans Albert Einstein, quoted in an interview with Bernard Mayer, in Whitrow, *Einstein*, p. 21

He often told me that one of the most important things in his life was music. Whenever he felt he had come to the end of the road or into a difficult situation in his work, he would take refuge in music and that would usually resolve all his difficulties.

Ibid.

When one was with him on the sailboat, you felt him as an element. He had something so natural and strong in him because he was himself a piece of nature. . . . He sailed like Odysseus.

Margot Einstein, May 4, 1978, in an interview with J. Sayen, in Sayen, *Einstein in America*, p. 132

No other man contributed so much to the vast expansion of twentieth-century knowledge.

Statement by President Dwight D. Eisenhower upon Einstein's death; quoted in the *New York Times*, April 19, 1955

Einstein's conversation was often a combination of inoffensive jokes and penetrating ridicule so that some people could not decide whether to laugh or to feel hurt. . . . Such an attitude often appeared to be an incisive criticism, and sometimes even created an impression of cynicism.

Philipp Frank, in Frank, *Einstein: His Life and Times*, p. 77

He, who had always had something of a bohemian in him, began to lead a middle-class life . . . in a household such as was typical of a well-to-do Berlin family. . . . When one entered . . . one found that Einstein still remained a "foreigner" in such a surrounding—a bohemian guest in a middle-class home.

Ibid. p. 124

Of course, the old man agrees with almost anything nowadays.

Cosmologist George Gamow, written on the bottom of a letter of August 4, 1948, from Einstein, after Einstein wrote him that one of Gamow's ideas was probably correct; in Reines, *Cosmology, Fusion and Other Matters*, p. 310

A man distinguished by his desire, if possible, to efface himself and yet impelled by the unmistakable power of genius which would not allow the individual of whom it had taken possession to rest for one moment.

Lord Haldane, London *Times*, June 14, 1921

We salute the new Columbus of science voyaging alone through the strange seas of thought.

President Hibben of Princeton University, upon conferring on Einstein an honorary doctorate, May 9, 1921; quoted in Frank, *Einstein: His Life and Times*, p. 183

The essence of Einstein's profundity lay in his simplicity; and the essence of his science lay in his artistry—his phenomenal sense of beauty.

Banesh Hoffmann, in Hoffmann, *Albert Einstein: Creator and Rebel*, p. 3

Einstein, with his feeling of humility, awe, and wonder, and his sense of oneness with the universe, belongs with the great religious mystics.

Ibid., p. 94

When it became clear that [we could not solve a problem], Einstein would stand up quietly and say, in his quaint English, "I vill a little t'ink." So saying he would pace up and down or walk around in circles, all the time twirling a lock of his long, graying hair around his finger.

Banesh Hoffmann, recollection quoted in Whitrow, *Einstein*, p. 75

The "Great Relative."

Name given Einstein by Hopi Indians on his visit to the United States, 1921; recounted in A&E Television Einstein Biography, VPI International, 1991

Einstein gave his wife the greatest care and sympathy. But in this atmosphere of coming death, Einstein remained serene and worked constantly.

Leopold Infeld, on Einstein's coping with wife Elsa's terminal illness of heart and kidney disease, in Infeld, *The Quest*, p. 282

The greatness of Einstein lies in his tremendous imagination, in the unbelievable obstinacy with which he pursues his problems.

Ibid., p. 208

If Einstein were to enter your room at a party and he were introduced to you as a "Mr. Eisenstein" of whom you knew nothing, you would still be fascinated by the brilliance of his eyes, by his shyness and gentleness, by his delightful sense of humor, by the fact that he can twist platitudes into wisdom. . . . You feel that before you is a man who thinks for himself. . . . He believes what you tell him because he is kind, because he wishes to be kind, and because it is much easier to believe than to disbelieve.

Leopold Infeld, in Infeld, *Albert Einstein*, p. 128

With all his phenomenal intellect, he is still a naive and altogether spontaneous human being.

Erich Kahler, 1954; Einstein Archive 38-279

Jewish physics can best and most justly be characterized by recalling the activity of one who is probably its most prominent representative, the pure-blooded Jew, Albert Einstein. His relativity theory was supposed to transform all of physics, but when faced with reality it did not have a leg to stand on. In contrast to the intractable and solicitous desire for truth in the Aryan scientist, the Jew lacks to a striking degree any comprehension of truth.

German physicist and Nobel laureate Philip Lenard, in his book, *German Physics* (1936)

Anyone who advises Americans to keep secret information which they may have about spies and saboteurs is himself an enemy of America.

Senator Joseph McCarthy, regarding Einstein's advocacy of refusing to testify at the House Un-American Activities Committee hearings; *New York Times*, June 14, 1953

For his unique services to theoretical physics and in particular for his discovery of the law of the photoelectric effect.

Nobel Prize Committee, official citation for the Nobel Prize in Physics, 1921

He has a quiet way of walking, as if he is afraid of alarming the truth and frightening it away.

Japanese cartoonist Ippei Okamoto on Einstein's visit to Japan, November 1922; see manuscript, "Einstein's 1922 Visit to Japan," in Einstein Archive 36-409 to 36-516

He was almost wholly without sophistication and wholly without worldliness. . . . There was always with him a wonderful purity at once childlike and profoundly stubborn.

Robert Oppenheimer, "On Albert Einstein," *New York Review of Books*, March 17, 1966

He responded with one of the most extraordinary kinds of laughter. . . . It was rather like the barking of a seal. It was a happy laughter. From that time on, I would save a good story for our next meeting, for the sheer pleasure of Einstein's laugh.

Abraham Pais, quoted in Bernstein, *Einstein*, p. 77

What Einstein said wasn't all that stupid.

Wolfgang Pauli as a student, after hearing Einstein, twenty years his senior, give a lecture; quoted in Ehlers, *Liebes Hertz!* p. 47

Doctor with the bushy head
Tell us that you're not a Red
Tell us that you do not eat
Capitalists in the street.
Say to us it isn't true
You devour their children too.
Speak, oh speak, and say you're notsky
Just a bent-space type of Trotsky.

> Verse written by popular newspaper columnist H. I. Phillips during the McCarthy era, poking fun at anti-Communist opposition to Einstein's entering the United States two decades earlier; quoted by Norman F. Stanley in *Physics Today*, November 1995, p. 118

Einstein loved women, and the commoner and sweatier and smellier they were, the better he liked them.

> Peter Plesch, quoting his father, János, in Highfield and Carter, *The Private Lives of Albert Einstein*, p. 206

What we must particularly admire in him is the facility with which he adapts himself to new concepts and knows how to draw from them every conclusion.

> Henri Poincaré, 1911, quoted in Hoffmann, *Albert Einstein: Creator and Rebel*, p. 99

Einstein was indisputably one of the greatest men of our time. He had, in a high degree, the simplicity characteristic of the best men of science—a simplicity which comes of a singleminded desire to know and understand things that are completely impersonal.

Bertrand Russell, in *The New Leader*, May 30, 1955

He removed the mystery from gravitation, which everybody since Newton had accepted with a reluctant feeling that it was unintelligible.

Bertrand Russell; quoted in Whitrow, *Einstein*, p. 22

Of all the public figures that I have known, Einstein was the one who commanded my most wholehearted admiration. . . . Einstein was not only a great scientist, he was a great man. He stood for peace in a world drifting towards war. He remained sane in a mad world, and liberal in a world of fanatics.

Ibid., p. 90

Even though without writing each other, we are in mental communication for we respond to our dreadful times in the same way and tremble together for the future of mankind. . . . I like it that we have the same given name.

Albert Schweitzer, letter of February 20, 1955; Einstein Archive 33-236

Tell Einstein I said the most convincing proof I can adduce of my admiration for him is that his is the only one of these portraits [of celebrities] I paid for.

George Bernard Shaw, recalled by Archibald Henderson, August 21, 1955, in the *Durham Morning Herald*; Einstein Archive 33-257 (Einstein's reply: "That is very characteristic of Bernard Shaw, who has declared that money is the most important thing in the world")

Ptolemy made a universe, which lasted 1400 years. Newton, also, made a universe, which lasted 300 years. Einstein has made a universe, and I can't tell you how long that will last.

George Bernard Shaw, at a banquet in England honoring Einstein; quoted in Cassidy, *Einstein and Our World*, p. 1; also shown in the Einstein film produced by Nova Television, 1979

To me, he appears as out of comparison the greatest intellect of this century, and almost certainly the greatest personification of moral experience. He was in many ways different from the rest of the species.

C. P. Snow, in *Conversations with Einstein*, as quoted in French, *Einstein: A Centenary Volume*, p. 193

He was a Zionist on general humanitarian grounds rather than on nationalistic grounds. He felt that Zionism was the only way in which the Jewish problem in Europe could be settled. . . . He was never in favor of aggressive nationalism, but he felt that a Jewish homeland in Palestine was essential to save the remaining Jews in Europe. . . . After the State of Israel was established, he said that somehow he felt happy he was not there to be involved in the deviations from the high moral tone he detected.

Ernst Straus, quoted in Whitrow, *Einstein*, pp. 87–88

One of the greatest—perhaps the greatest—of achievements in the history of human thought.

Joseph John Thomson, discoverer of the electron, referring to Einstein's work on general relativity, 1919; quoted in Hoffmann, *Albert Einstein: Creator and Rebel*, p. 132

Einstein was a physicist and not a philosopher. But the naive directness of his questions was philosophical.

C. F. von Weizsaecker, quoted in Aichenburg and Sexl, *Albert Einstein*, p. 159

Einstein explained his theory to me every day, and soon I was fully convinced that he understood it.

Chaim Weizmann, 1929

Einstein's [violin] playing is excellent, but he does not deserve his world fame; there are many others just as good.

> A Berlin music critic on an early 1920s performance, unaware that Einstein's fame derived from physics, not music; quoted in Reiser, *Albert Einstein*, pp. 202–203

"Prof. Einstein's Got a New Baby: Formula Keeps Our Man Up Nights."

> Headline of a book review of *The Meaning of Relativity* which appeared in the *Daily Mirror* (New York), March 30, 1953; it referred to the appendix published two years before Einstein's death in which he presented a greatly simplified derivation of the equations of general relativity. (Contributed by Trevor Lipscombe)

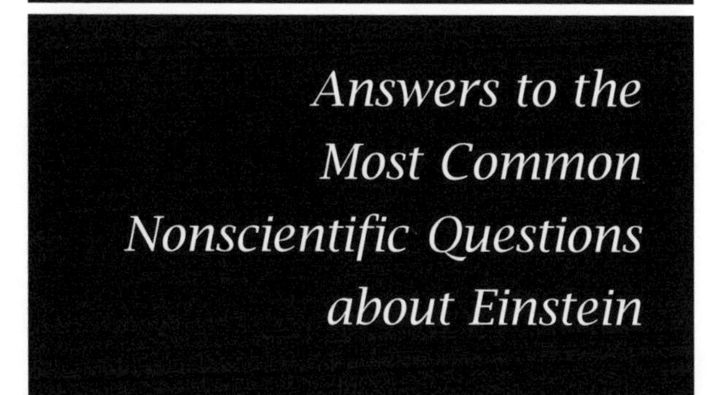

Answers to the Most Common Nonscientific Questions about Einstein

Playing the violin, 1929. (Ullstein Bilderdienst, Berlin)

This information has been culled from various sources in the Einstein archive and in the published literature. Much of it can be found in the standard good biographies of Einstein, such as those by Abraham Pais, Jamie Sayen, and Philipp Frank.

PHYSICISTS EINSTEIN ADMIRED THE MOST

Michael Faraday, James Clerk Maxwell, and Isaac Newton.

PHILOSOPHERS WHO INFLUENCED HIM THE MOST

David Hume, for his criticism of traditional commonsense assumptions and dogmas; Ernst Mach, for his criticism of Newton's ideas concerning space, for his critical examination of Newtonian mechanics, and for his encouragement of intellectual skepticism; Spinoza, for his views on religion; and Schopenhauer, for the inspirational "A man can do what he wants, but not want what he wants." (See Frank, *Einstein: His Life and Times*, p. 52; Whitrow, *Einstein*, pp. 12–13; *Ideas and Opinions*, p. 8)

BOOKS AND AUTHORS HE ENJOYED

Gandhi's autobiography; John Hersey's *A Bell for Adano* and *The Wall*; books by Dostoevsky, Tolstoi, and Herodotus; Spinoza's writings on religion. Books on science that he recommended in 1920 were Weyl's *Time, Space, Matter* and Schlick's *Space and Time in Physics Today,* along with another volume entitled *The Principle of Relativity,* whose third edition was to contain the most important of the original essays on general relativity. (See Einstein's letter to Maurice Solovine, April 24, 1920, in *Letters to Solovine,* p. 31)

HIS FAVORITE MUSIC AND COMPOSERS

Bach, Mozart, and some old Italian and English composers were Einstein's favorites; also Schubert, because of the composer's ability to express emotion. He was considerably less fond of Beethoven, regarding his music as too dramatic and personal. Handel, he felt, was technically good but displayed shallowness. Schumann's shorter works were attractive because they were original and rich in feeling. Mendelssohn had considerable talent but lacked depth. He liked some *lieder* and chamber music by Brahms. He found Wagner's musical personality indescribably offensive "so that for the most part I can listen to him only with disgust." He considered Richard Strauss gifted but without inner truth and concerned too much with outside effect.

(From a response to a questionnaire, 1939; Einstein Archive 34-322)

Einstein began to play the violin at age six; by 1950 he had given it up and instead played around on the piano. He had called his violin "Lina" and willed it to his grandson Bernhard. (Frank, *Einstein: His Life and Times*, p. 14; Grüning, *Ein Haus für Albert Einstein*, p. 251)

HOBBIES

Besides music and reading, Einstein's other passion was sailing. For his fiftieth birthday, a group of friends bought him a sailboat, which he sailed on the Havel River at his summer home in Caputh, southwest of Berlin. The boat was called *Tummler* ("acrobat"). Later, in Princeton, he sailed on Lake Carnegie in his boat *Tinnef* ("cheaply made" in Yiddish).

HANDEDNESS

Einstein, unlike many physicists and mathematicians, was right-handed. See photos showing him pointing with his right finger (p. 133) and holding a pen in his right hand (e.g., the photo with Robert Oppenheimer on p. 119). He also held the bow to his violin in the right hand (p. 243), though admittedly some left-handed people do this as well. No one ever referred to his left-handedness, which would have been unusual in the life of a left-handed person.

UNDERSTANDING RELATIVITY THEORY

Einstein denied that he ever made the assertion that only twelve people in the world could understand his theory. He thought that every physicist who studied the theory could readily understand it. (Denial made to reporters upon his arrival in New York in 1921; see Frank, *Einstein: His Life and Times*, p. 179)

EINSTEIN'S AMERICAN CITIZENSHIP

Einstein entered the United States in 1933 with only a visitor's visa. Under U.S. immigration law at the time, permission to become a citizen could be obtained only through an American consul in a foreign country. Einstein therefore chose to go to Bermuda to apply for citizenship in May 1935. The American consul threw a gala dinner in his honor and gave him permission to enter the United States as a permanent resident. Five years later, in 1940, he, Margot Einstein, and Helen Dukas became citizens as they took their oath of U.S. allegiance in Trenton, New Jersey. (See Pais, *Einstein Lived Here*, p. 199, and Frank, *Einstein: His Life and Times*, p. 293, though Frank gives the wrong year of citizenship)

AT THE INSTITUTE FOR ADVANCED STUDY

Einstein's starting salary at the Institute for Advanced Study in Princeton in 1933 was $15,000 per year, with a $5,000 yearly pension at retirement (Einstein Archive 29-315). The Institute was given temporary quarters on the Princeton University campus, in a part of the old mathematics building, Fine Hall (now Jones Hall, location of the East Asian Studies department), until 1940, when it was moved to its own campus in a rural part of Princeton. Einstein retired in 1945 but continued to occupy an office at the Institute until his death.

At the time, Abraham Flexner was the director of the Institute and, to Einstein's annoyance, proved to be an overly protective boss. Soon after Einstein's arrival in the United States, for example, President Roosevelt invited Einstein and his wife, Elsa—via the director's office—to the White House. Flexner took it upon himself to decline the invitation without consulting Einstein, citing security reasons. Sometime later, Einstein was told about this incident and hastily wrote an apologetic letter to Roosevelt. The invitation was extended once again, and Einstein finally did go to the White House to meet the president.

EINSTEIN'S DEATH

Einstein died at Princeton Hospital on April 18, 1955 (see Chronology).

His brain and eyes were removed and preserved, to be saved for future study (see Highfield and Carter, *The Private Lives of Albert Einstein*, pp. 264ff; *The Guardian* [London], December 17, 1994; *California Monthly*, December 1995, pp. 27–28). The pathologist, Dr. Thomas Harvey, performed an autopsy and, without permission, removed the brain and kept it. Another pathologist, Dr. Henry Abrams, took the eyes with permission of the hospital administrator, receiving a letter of authenticity from Dr. Guy Dean, Einstein's personal physician at the time of death. Einstein's family did not know this was being done. He had asked that his body be cremated, and the removal of the organs was considered by Einstein's friends to be a violation of his wishes. After the cremation, the Einstein family learned about the brain and agreed to let Dr. Harvey keep it if he did not use it for commercial purposes but only for scientific study. He has given at least three parts to other scientists, but only Dr. Marian Diamond of the University of California at Berkeley has made a scientific contribution, reporting in 1985 in *Experimental Neurology* that Einstein's brain has an above-average number of glial cells (which nourish neurons) in those areas of the left hemisphere that are thought to control mathematical and linguistic skills. An enlarged image of Einstein's glial cells is on view at the Lawrence Hall of Science in Berkeley.

Einstein's body was cremated in Trenton on the day of his death, and his ashes were scattered by two friends, Otto Nathan and Paul Oppenheim. The last person to see Einstein alive was nurse Alberta Rozsel, who reported, "He gave two breaths and expired" (*New York Times*, April 19, 1955).

A memorial concert took place at McCarter Theater in Princeton on December 17, 1955, and featured the following program: R. Casadesus, piano, and the Princeton University Orchestra performing Mozart's Coronation Concerto (concerto for piano and orchestra in D Major) and Bach's Sonatina from Cantata no. 106 "Actus Tragicus." Also played were Haydn's Symphony no. 104 in D Major and Corelli's Concerto Grosso no. 8 ("Christmas").

MISCELLANEOUS PERSONAL INFORMATION

Einstein did not learn to speak until he was three years old. It has been suggested that this lateness was the origin of his thinking in visual terms (i.e., his "thought experiments").

Einstein was a better than average student in school. His highest marks were in mathematics, physics, and music. His lowest were in French and Italian. (*CPAE*, Vol. 1, Docs. 8 and 10)

Einstein's Swiss military service book shows the following result of a health examination that deemed him unfit for military service at the age of 22 (March 13, 1901):

> Body height, 171.5 cm (5 ft, 7.6 in)
> Chest circumference, 87 cm (34.8 in)
> Upper arm, 28 cm (11.2 in)
> Diseases or defects: varicose veins, flat feet, and excessive foot perspiration

(see *CPAE*, Vol. 1, Doc. 91). According to Helen Dukas, Einstein was required to pay a tax until 1940 for not serving in the Swiss military; he kept a *Dienstbuch* (service book) from the military that showed yearly entries of tax payments.

In 1920, Einstein asked Princeton University for a $15,000 honorarium for two months of lecturing, three lectures a week (Einstein Archive 36-241). However, the Princeton lectures, delivered in 1921 and published in 1922, were cut down to four lectures entitled "The Meaning of Relativity," for which he received a much smaller fee.

Einstein generally wrote short letters, which were to the point, especially in his later years. The longest handwritten letter he wrote: ten pages to physicist H. A. Lorentz on January 23, 1915. (Einstein Archive 16-436)

He claimed he got his hairstyle "through negligence."

Einstein and his family were animal lovers. In Princeton they kept a cat named Tiger and a dog named Chico.

Einstein did not like to have his manuscripts reviewed. In the summer of 1936 he submitted a paper to the *Physical Review*, and a referee returned it with ten pages of comments. Insulted, Einstein withdrew the paper so he could publish it elsewhere. He claimed the *Physical Review* had no right to show the paper to reviewers before publication, as was (and is) the American custom. (Letter to the editor of the *Physical Review*, July 27, 1936; Einstein Archive 19-087)

Grete Markstein, a talented actress, claimed to be Einstein's daughter until the day she died. To disprove her claim, Einstein, on Helen Dukas's initiative, had her birth records checked, and they proved otherwise (for example, she was only thirteen years younger than he). She died in 1947. (From notes of a conversation with Helen Dukas.) Both Einstein and his friend János Plesch have written humorous poems about Mrs. Markstein (Einstein Archive 31-540 and 31-541).

Einstein never allowed his name to be used for commercial advertising, though he received some curious requests, for example, from a hair restorer and a soap manufacturer; also from a maker of pens. If he showed enthusiasm for a product, word would get around and he would be approached to endorse and promote it. Today his estate employs a California-based advertising agency to preserve commercial use of his name with a trademark.

By middle and old age, Einstein came to harbor bitter feelings against the opposite sex, calling marriage incompatible with human nature: marriage makes people treat each other as property and one can no longer operate as a free human being. All the men in Einstein's nuclear family preferred older women as partners: both of Einstein's wives were at least three years older than he; son Hans Albert's first wife was nine years older, the second wife two years older; son Eduard had an older woman friend, though he never married.

Einstein snored "unbelievably loudly," according to Elsa, so they kept separate bedrooms. Elsa was not allowed to enter his study—he demanded complete privacy there. To Elsa: "Speak of you *or* me, but never of 'us.'" He wanted complete independence, never using "we" with his wife and not allowing her to speak for him, either.

Bibliography

Aichenburg, P., and R. Sexl. *Albert Einstein*. Braunschweig: Vieweg, 1979.

Bernstein, Jeremy. *Einstein*. New York: Penguin, 1978.

Born, Max, ed. *Einstein-Born Briefwechsel, 1916–1955*. Munich: Nymphenbürger, 1969.

———. *The Born-Einstein Letters*. London: Macmillan, 1971.

Cassidy, David. *Einstein and Our World*. Atlantic Highlands, N.J.: Humanities Press, 1995.

Clark, Ronald W. *Einstein: The Life and Times*. New York: Crowell, 1971.

Cline, Barbara Lovett. *Men Who Made a New Physics*. Chicago: University of Chicago Press, 1987.

CPAE. See Stachel et al. for Vols. 1 and 2; Klein et al. for Vol. 5; Schulmann et al. for Vol. 8.

Cuny, Hilaire. *Albert Einstein: The Man and His Times*. London, 1963.

Dukas, Helen, and Banesh Hoffman. *Albert Einstein, the Human Side*. Princeton, N.J.: Princeton University Press, 1979.

Dürrenmatt, Friedrich. *Albert Einstein: Ein Vortrag*. Zurich: Diogenes, 1979.

Ehlers, Anita. *Liebes Hertz!* Berlin: Birkhäuser, 1994.

Einstein, Albert. *About Zionism*. Trans. L. Simon. New York: Macmillan, 1931.

———. *The World as I See It*. Abridged ed. New York: Philosophical Library, n.d.; distributed by Citadel Press. Orig. in Leach, *Living Philosophies*, 1931.

———. *The Origins of the Theory of Relativity*. Glasgow: Jackson, Wylie, 1933.

———. *Mein Weltbild*. Amsterdam: Querido Verlag, 1934.

Einstein, Albert. *Out of My Later Years*. Paperback ed. New York: Wisdom Library of the Philosophical Library, 1950. (Other editions exist as well; page numbers refer to this edition.)

———. *Ideas and Opinions*. Trans. Sonja Bargmann. New York: Crown, 1954. (Other editions exist as well; page numbers refer to this edition.)

———. *Albert Einstein/Mileva Marić*: The Love Letters. Ed. Jürgen Renn and Robert Schulmann. Trans. Shawn Smith. Princeton, N.J.: Princeton University Press, 1992.

———. *Einstein on Humanism*. New York: Carol Publishing, 1993.

———. *Letters to Solovine, 1906–1955*. Trans. from the French by Wade Baskin, with facsimile letters in German. New York: Carol Publishing, 1993.

Einstein, Albert, and Sigmund Freud. *Why War?* Paris: Institute of Intellectual Cooperation, League of Nations, 1933.

Einstein, Albert, and Leopold Infeld. *The Evolution of Physics*. New York: Simon and Schuster, 1938.

Einstein: A Portrait. Corte Madera, Calif.: Pomegranate Artbooks, 1984.

Frank, Philipp. *Einstein: His Life and Times*. New York: Knopf, 1947, 1953.

———. *Einstein: Sein Leben und seine Zeit*. Braunschweig: Vieweg, 1979.

French, A. P., ed. *Einstein: A Centenary Volume*. Cambridge, Mass.: Harvard University Press, 1979.

Grüning, Michael. *Ein Haus für Albert Einstein*. Berlin: Verlag der Nation, 1990.

Hadamard, Jacques. *An Essay on the Psychology of Invention in the Mathematical Field*. Princeton, N.J.: Princeton University Press, 1945.

Highfield, Roger, and Paul Carter. *The Private Lives of Albert Einstein*. London: Faber and Faber, 1993.

Hoffmann, Banesh. *Albert Einstein: Creator and Rebel*. New York: Viking, 1972.

———. "Einstein and Zionism." In *General Relativity and Gravitation*, ed. G. Shaviv and J. Rosen. New York: Wiley, 1975.

Holton, Gerald. *The Advancement of Science, and Its Burdens.* New York: Cambridge University Press, 1986.

Holton, Gerald, and Yehuda Elkana, eds. *Albert Einstein: Historical and Cultural Perspectives. The Centennial Symposium in Jerusalem.* Princeton, N.J.: Princeton University Press, 1982.

Infeld, Leopold. *The Quest: The Evolution of a Scientist.* New York: Doubleday, 1941.

———. *Albert Einstein.* Rev. ed. New York: Charles Scribner's Sons, 1950.

Klein, Martin, A. J. Kox, and Robert Schulmann, eds. *The Collected Papers of Albert Einstein,* Vol. 5, *The Swiss Years: Correspondence, 1902–1914.* Princeton, N.J.: Princeton University Press, 1993. (Trans. Anna Beck, 1995.)

Leach, Henry J., ed. *Living Philosophies: A Series of Intimate Credos.* New York: Simon and Schuster, 1931.

Michelmore, P. *Einstein: Profile of the Man.* New York: Dodd, 1962.

Moszkowski, Alexander. *Conversations with Einstein.* Trans. Henry L. Brose. New York: Horizon Press, 1970. (Conversations took place in 1920, trans. 1921, published 1970.)

Nathan, Otto, and Heinz Norden, eds. *Einstein on Peace.* New York: Simon and Schuster, 1960. (Other editions exist as well; page numbers refer to this edition.)

Pais, Abraham. *Subtle Is the Lord: The Science and the Life of Albert Einstein.* Oxford: Oxford University Press, 1982.

———. *Einstein Lived Here.* Oxford: Oxford University Press, 1994.

Planck, Max. *Where Is Science Going?* New York: Norton, 1932.

Regis, Ed. *Who Got Einstein's Office?* Reading, Mass.: Addison-Wesley, 1987.

Reines, Frederick, ed. *Cosmology, Fusion and Other Matters. A Memorial to George Gamow.* Boulder: University Press of Colorado, 1972.

Reiser, Anton. *Albert Einstein: A Biographical Portrait.* New York: Boni, 1930.

Rosenthal-Schneider, Ilse. *Reality and Scientific Truth*. Detroit: Wayne State University Press, 1980.

Ryan, Dennis P., ed. *Einstein and the Humanities*. New York: Greenwood Press, 1987.

Sayen, Jamie. *Einstein in America*. New York: Crown, 1985.

Schilpp, Paul, ed. *Albert Einstein: Philosopher-Scientist*. Evanston, Ill.: Library of Living Philosophers, 1949.

———, ed. and trans. *Albert Einstein: Autobiographical Notes*. Paperback ed. La Salle, Ill.: Open Court, 1979.

Schulmann, Robert, et al., eds. *The Collected Papers of Albert Einstein*, Vol. 8, *The Berlin Years: Correspondence, 1914–1918*. Princeton, N.J.: Princeton University Press, 1997 (forthcoming).

Seelig, Carl, ed. *Helle Zeit, Dunkle Zeit: In Memoriam Albert Einstein*. Zurich: Europa Verlag, 1956.

Stachel, John, et al., eds. *The Collected Papers of Albert Einstein*, Vol. 1, *The Early Years: 1879–1902*. Princeton, N.J.: Princeton University Press, 1987. (Trans. Anna Beck, 1987.)

———. *The Collected Papers of Albert Einstein*, Vol. 2, *The Swiss Years: Writings, 1900–1909*. Princeton, N.J.: Princeton University Press, 1989. (Trans. Anna Beck, 1989.)

Vallentin, Antonina. *Das Drama Albert Einsteins*. Stuttgart: Günther Verlag, 1955.

Whitrow, G. J. *Einstein: The Man and His Achievement*. New York: Dover, 1967.

Index of Key Words

Subject Index

ALICE CALAPRICE is the in-house editor of Princeton University Press's *The Collected Papers of Albert Einstein* and the administrator of its translation project. She is a senior editor specializing in science manuscripts and is the recipient of the 1995 LMP Award for Individual Editorial Achievement in Scholarly Publishing.